Air Fryer Cookbook

600 Days Delicious, Easy & Effortless Recipes for Family and Busy People

Janet M. Guy

Copyright© 2022 By Janet M. Guy All Rights Reserved

This book is copyright protected. It is only for personal use. You cannot amend, distribute, sell, use, quote or paraphrase any part of the content within this book, without the consent of the author or publisher.

Under no circumstances will any blame or legal responsibility be held against the publisher, or author, for any damages, reparation, or monetary loss due to the information contained within this book, either directly or indirectly.

Disclaimer Notice:

Please note the information contained within this document is for educational and entertainment purposes only. All effort has been executed to present accurate, up to date, reliable, complete information. No warranties of any kind are declared or implied. Readers acknowledge that the author is not engaged in the rendering of legal, financial, medical or professional advice. The content within this book has been derived from various sources. Please consult a licensed professional before attempting any techniques outlined in this book.

By reading this document, the reader agrees that under no circumstances is the author responsible for any losses, direct or indirect, that are incurred as a result of the use of the information contained within this document, including, but not limited to, errors, omissions, or inaccuracies.

Table of Contents

Introduction 1

Getting to know the air fryer 2

Food to cook and to avoid 3

What not to cook in an air fryer 4

Eight Benefits of an air fryer 4

Possible Risks 6

  How to clean an air fryer 6

  Tips and Tricks 7

Chapter 1 Breakfasts 9

  Peppe Spinach Omelet 9

  Veggie Frittata 9

  Breakfast Pita 9

  Cheesy Cauliflower "Hash Browns" 10

  Gold Avocado 10

  Baked Peach Oatmeal 11

  Bunless Breakfast Turkey Burgers 11

  Hole in One 11

  Banana-Nut Muffins 12

  Breakfast Meatballs 12

  Sausage and Egg Breakfast Burrito 13

  Broccoli-Mushroom Frittata 13

  Bacon Muffin Sandwiches 14

  Breakfast Calzone 14

  Creamy Cinnamon Rolls 15

  Mozzarella Bacon Calzones 15

Chapter 2 Fish and seafood 17

New Orleans-Style Crab Cakes 17

Apple Cider Mussels 17

Crab-Stuffed Avocado Boats 17

Tuna and Fruit Kebabs 18

Southern-Style Catfish 18

Smoky Prawn and Chorizo Tapas 18

Crab Legs 19

Snapper Scampi 19

Tilapia Sandwiches with Tartar Sauce 20

Oregano Tilapia Fingers 20

Almond-Crusted Fish 21

Marinated Salmon Fillets 21

Sweet Tilapia Fillets 22

Chapter 3 Poultry 23

Fried Chicken Breasts 23

Chicken Schnitzel Dogs 23

Chicken Breasts with Asparagus, Beans, and Rocket 24

Crisp Paprika Chicken Drumsticks 24

Thai-Style Cornish Game Hens 25

Smoky Chicken Leg Quarters 25

Golden Chicken Cutlets 26

Pork Scratching Fried Chicken 26

Bacon Lovers' Stuffed Chicken 26

'Bacon-Wrapped Stuffed Chicken Breasts 27

Chapter 4 Vegetables and Sides 28

Green Tomato Salad 28

Kohlrabi Fries 28

Curried Fruit 29

Hasselback Potatoes with Chive Pesto 29

Asparagus Fries 30

Indian Aubergine Bharta 30

Spiced Butternut Squash 30

Roasted Brussels Sprouts with Bacon...31

Roasted Sweet Potatoes 31

Radish Chips 31

Mashed Sweet Potato Tots 32

Parsnip Fries with Romesco Sauce 32

Garlic-Parmesan Crispy Baby Potatoes 33

Garlic Roasted Broccoli 33

Chermoula-Roasted Beets 34

Chapter 5 Beef, Pork, and Lamb 35

Mongolian-Style Beef 35

Beef and Tomato Sauce Meatloaf 35

Sichuan Cumin Lamb 36

Sausage and Peppers 36

Bacon-Wrapped Pork Tenderloin 37

Herb-Crusted Lamb Chops 37

Spaghetti Zoodles and Meatballs 38

Garlic Balsamic Beef 38

Beef Burger..39

Bacon, Cheese and Pear Stuffed Pork 39

Pork Medallions with Radicchio and Endive Salad 40

Smothered Chops 41

Air Fryer Chicken-Fried Steak 41

Herb-Roasted Beef Tips with Onions 42

Blackened Cajun Pork Roast 42

Bacon-Wrapped Cheese Pork 43

Pork Tenderloin with Avocado Lime Sauce 43

Chapter 6 Snacks and Appetisers... 45

Aubergine Fries 45

Crispy Breaded Beef Cubes 45

Shishito Peppers with Herb Dressing ... 46

Carrot Chips ... 46

Crunchy Tex-Mex Tortilla Chips ... 46

Lemony Endive in Curried Yogurt ... 47

Lemon-Pepper Chicken Drumsticks ... 47

Cheesy Steak Fries ... 48

Black Bean Corn Dip ... 48

Golden Onion Rings ... 49

Bruschetta with Basil Pesto ... 50

Stuffed Figs with Goat Cheese and Honey ... 50

Courgette Fries with Roasted Garlic Aïoli ... 50

Dark Chocolate and Cranberry Granola Bars ... 51

Caramelised Onion Dip ... 52

Ranch Oyster Snack Crackers ... 52

Lemony Pear Chips ... 52

Crunchy Chickpeas ... 53

Classic Spring Rolls ... 53

Asian Five-Spice Wings ... 54

Old Bay Chicken Wings ... 54

Chapter 7 Desserts ... 56

Cinnamon and Pecan Pie ... 56

Olive Oil Cake ... 56

Rhubarb and Strawberry Crumble ... 56

Blackberry Cobbler ... 57

Apple Hand Pies ... 57

Gingerbread ... 58

Lime Bars ... 59

Bananas Foster ... 59

Frozen Air Fryer Pancakes ... 59

Air fryer Banana Souffle: ... 60

Grilled Air Fryer Peaches: ... 60

Introduction

Fish and chips, scotch eggs, fried chicken. For almost all of British history, the only way to have those foods would be if they were deep fried in oil (or lard in the past) bought from a takeaway shop.

Today, however, not only are people able to enjoy these, and many more, fantastic meals, we can do so for a fraction of the price and with a fraction of the saturated fat.

And that's possible because of the newest piece of kitchen tech- the air fryer! This book will look at what an air fryer is, why people love them so much, and what you can make with them.

Why I love my air fryer

Later in this e-book, I will go into far more detail about what I love so much about my air fryer, but in short, you can make delicious, quick, and healthy meals.

Restaurant quality food doesn't require much money on expensive cooking equipment or drowning your food in a deep fat fryer.

Even if you have a small kitchen, you can take your cooking to a new level with your air fryer.

As a professional chef, I work very hard in the kitchen all day, making some meals that took years of training. However, I don't want work to continue when I get home. I love throwing some fresh but simple ingredients into my air fryer and creating something magnificent.

Why I wrote this cookbook

Although I have had my air fryer for about 5 years now, it was only a couple of months ago that I decided to write this book.

When I bought my air fryer, it was a new and novel way of cooking meals. Today, however, it seems as though almost everyone has one. Perhaps this is because takeaways are becoming more expensive, or maybe it's because people are becoming more aware of the health dangers of deep-fried foods.

But, I wanted to write this e-book to show that anyone can cook with an air fryer. And when I say "cook", I mean cook properly.

I am rather fed up with these "tik tok chefs" air frying ingredients such as frozen meats, American cheese, and chemical-laden bread. I want to show that the air fryer isn't some internet fad but the next stage of cooking technology.

What I hope this book will give you

Hopefully, by the end of this book, you will have the confidence to use your air fryer to make delicious and healthy meals. Be that healthy recreations of your favourite takeaways, traditional hearty meals, or new and adventurous dishes.

Yes, I am a professional chef with 20 years of experience, but you don't need to be. What I love about the air fryer is its simple and easy use!

After reading this e-book, I would encourage you to seek out new recipes or to try creating your own.

Getting to know the air fryer

The air fryer is an incredible piece of technology. Using just one spoonful of oil, you can create similar effects to a large tub of oil!
This chapter will examine how it works and why it's better than a deep fat fryer!

How does an air fryer work

An air fryer is essentially an enclosed convection oven.
Directly above your food is a heating element, which sends heat, via infrared radiation, downwards onto your food. But, what makes an air fryer different from a grill is the addition of the fan above the element.
The fan moves the hot air throughout the food- pushing hot air to the bottom, where it needs to pass through the food to rise to the top again.
An air guide (usually shaped like a starfish) at the bottom of your air fryer distributes the hot air evenly. It ensures it reaches all parts of the food. The fact that your food is heated from all directions gives air-fried food a similar quality to fried foods.
At the top, you'll find an exhaust, which releases a little air if the device gets too hot.

The (health) dangers of deep frying

Most people are aware that air frying uses significantly less fat than deep frying. But, have you ever wondered why fat is so bad for you?
Well, the truth is, not all fat is bad. But Trans Fats and saturated fats certainly are.
These fats increase your body's cholesterol- a thin layer of fat in our arteries. Cholesterol, in moderation, is essential for insulation. But, having too much of it can clog the arteries, stopping blood from travelling around your body.
Foods high in trans fats can't get broken down quickly, so they stick to your arteries and increase your cholesterol levels.
High cholesterol can lead to many medical issues, including heart disease, diabetes, and obesity.
As a mother, I want my kids to live long and happy lives. I certainly do not want them to live a life of clogged arteries.
Deep-fried foods are some of the worst for cholesterol. Foods are often fried in oils such as canola, soy, corn, sunflower, and sesame. Cheap oil is highly saturated and challenging for the body to break down.
Sure, you could fry in olive oil or similar oils, but could you imagine how much that would cost?

The (safety) dangers of deep frying

As well as health reasons, there are also safety reasons not to get a deep fat fryer.
Did you know deep fat fryers cause 1000 fires a year, with about 5 deaths… just on Thanksgiving! I couldn't even find the data for how much damage they cause in a year!
Here are some more reasons why you should opt for an air fryer over a deep fryer.
- It's more energy efficient. A deep fryer uses 1800 kWhs, but an air fryer only uses 1500.
- Your food cooks faster as you don't need to wait for lots of oil to heat up.

Food to cook and to avoid

Scotch Eggs

In many countries, most people aren't familiar with the "scotch egg", but when I visited the UK, I absolutely fell in love with them.

Essentially the scotch egg is an egg (as the name suggests) coated in sausage meat, covered in bread crumbs, and then deep fried (or air fried in my case).

It's a super simple yet delicious recipe that anyone can make. It uses everyday ingredients that most of us will have lying around.

And you can get creative with it too! For example, I once had a scotch egg that used panko bread crumbs and another that used black pudding instead of pork meat.

If you have an air fryer, you can have delicious, fresh, hot scotch eggs whenever you want.

Doughnuts

Doughnuts are a delicious sweet treat. Whether ringed or filled, a doughnut is a fantastic treat for anyone! Whether you're eating them on the go with a cup of coffee or sitting down to enjoy them.

The two main problems with doughnuts are how much they cost and how unhealthy they are. But, making your own in the air fryer eliminates both these problems.

Air fryer doughnuts are cheaper and healthier than you get in the doughnut shop.

Breaded fish

Fish is a delicious, high-protein food that goes well with many things. Breaded fish is best if you're cooking it in the air fryer.

Once you've cooked your breaded fish, you can serve it with fries, in a roll, or with vegetables. The choice is yours.

And don't think you have to use cod. There are many types of fish: halibut, salmon, mackerel, place, and huss. You could even cook whatever kind of fish is in your local area.

Chicken

We all love fried chicken. The juicy tender chicken is covered in a crispy breadcrumb. And now, you don't need to rely on greasy fast food joints or unhealthy frozen chicken to enjoy the delicious treat.

When you cook your "fried" chicken in the air fryer, it's healthier and often crispier than what you would get in fast food joints. Plus, you can use whatever herbs and spices you like.

Falafel

Falafel is a fantastic middle eastern food made from chickpeas. It's soft, flavoursome, and surprisingly healthy. Falafel has all the protein of a burger, with a tiny fraction of the saturated fat.

Whether you're vegetarian, trying to be healthy, or just want to explore new foods, falafel is a brilliant way to start!

Usually, it's served in balls, but you can also get falafel burgers.

Chips/Fries

Crispy on the outside, soft in the middle. Chips (or fries) are a favourite part of many people's diets. Nothing beats a nice hot bowl of chips with your favourite dipping sauce.

When you cook them in the air fryer, you get the chip's crispiness from the deep fryer, with just a tiny fraction of the fat.

Once they're cooked, you eat them just the same! Be that with a burger, fish, fried chicken, or coated in sauce.

Roast Potatoes

Staying with the theme of potatoes, you can also make excellent roast potatoes in your air fryer. Cover them in oil, rosemary, thyme, or whatever herbs you want, and throw them into your air fryer.

Cooking roast potatoes in the air fryer makes them crispier and cooks them quicker than they would in the oven. If you're only cooking for one, heating a whole oven to cook a portion of potatoes is a waste of time.

Calamari

Calamari is one of the best ways to enjoy squid! They're rings of squid meat coated in breadcrumbs, Squid, like most fish, is an excellent source of protein and very easy to cook with!

What not to cook in an air fryer

That was what you SHOULD cook. But here's a quick list of what you shouldn't cook and why.
- Wet Batter- It doesn't set like it does in oil.
- Leafy Greens- They will burn and cook unevenly.
- Whole roast meats- Even if it fits, the bit by the heat sources will burn before the bottom is cooked.
- Cheese- Will burn and stick. It will be a nightmare to clean!
- Raw Grains- Air frying is dry cooking. If you cook dry grains, they will burn.
- Toast- The crumbs will blow everywhere, making the air fryer harder to clean.

Eight Benefits of an air fryer

If you don't yet have an air fryer and you're questioning if you should, this next chapter is for you! There are hundreds of reasons I love my air fryer, but in this chapter, I've picked the eight most important reasons to convince you to spend your money on an air fryer.

#1 It's much healthier.

We spoke in chapter one about why fat is bad for your arteries. But, when you air fry instead of deep fry, you use a tiny fraction of the oil you would use otherwise. Just one teaspoon is enough to cook your food to perfection.

In case you skipped chapter one, our body takes a long time to break down trans fats, which are commonly found in cooking oils. Since our body can't break it down, it stores the fat in the arteries, but too much, stopping the blood from flowing.

#2 Food becomes much Crispier.

We all love crispy food. Whether it's fries, chicken, scotch egg, or anything. It's always better when it has that lovely bit of bite. Cooking things in the oven is rarely the best way to make them crispy. It may get crispy on top, but the beautiful crispy coating is more difficult.

Have you tried making oven chips in the oven? They're never as crispy as you want them to be! Before the air fryer, deep frying was the only way to get crispy food.

Plus, the addition of the basket lets fat drip away, making your food even crispier.

#3 Air frying is quick.

When you're hungry, you want your food and you want it fast. The trouble with conventional cooking is that it often involves preheating.

Do you want to wait to heat up a whole oven? Or a tub of oil? I certainly don't.

Air frying is 30-50% quicker than cooking in an oven.

#4 There is less mess.

Many people (myself included) love cooking but hate washing up. Not even the air fryer can eliminate the need for washing up completely. However, it's much easier to clean than a traditional deep-fat fryer.

I have a friend who works in Mcdonald's, constantly complaining about how much work it is to clean a deep fryer.

A deep fat fryer needs to be cleaned regularly. The oil needs to get drained, and the trays must be scrubbed.

But, because the air fryer hardly uses any oil, cleaning is much simpler.

#5 It's much safer

Because the device is self-contained, there is no hot oil splashing. This means you won't need to worry about burning yourself or the oil splashing onto your kitchen.

Safety is super important. If you're deep frying and oil splashes onto your bare skin, you will be in great pain. In some cases, you may even require medical attention.

#6 It doesn't spread heat or odour

If you live in an apartment, the last thing you need is your whole house smelling like whatever you're frying. But, because the air fryer is enclosed, all the smells stay trapped.

#7 It's Smaller.

Most air fryers are about the size of a toaster. These can easily be set up on the kitchen counter.

No matter how small your kitchen is, you can use an air fryer. Its small size makes it great for all sorts of people- folk who travel a lot, folk in a caravan, folk in a small kitchen.

#8 It's easy to use.

All you need to do is set the time, set the temperature, and press "Start".

Then, just leave it alone. What you do whilst it's frying is up to you. Cook your sides, have a tea, write a poem. It's up to you.

There are, of course, plenty more benefits of an air fryer, but those are the eight I find most important.

Possible Risks

As great as air fryers are, nothing in this world is perfect. So, even if you decide to buy one, there are some things you ought to be aware of.

Please be aware this chapter is not designed to discourage you from buying an air fryer; the pros far outweigh the cons. However, it's still important to be aware of the risks before making this kind of investment.

It could (still) create harmful compounds

When you cook certain foods at high temperatures, you create certain chemicals that can increase the risk of cancer and other health-related illnesses.

If you cook with cheaper, saturated fats, consuming lots of food from your air fryer can still damage your arteries. Because there is less oil than deep frying, the health risks are lessened, but they are not entirely eliminated.

Extra research is still needed into how healthy air-fried food is- although most will agree it's far healthier than deep frying.

It's not 100% guaranteed to be healthy

We discussed the "Tik Tok Air Fryer Chef" in the introduction. People throw processed junk into their air fryers, such as frozen meats, processed cheese, and high-sodium ingredients.

Cooking this kind of food in an air fryer is better than a deep fryer, but a nacho-coated ball of processed hamburger meat with American cheese inside is not healthy, even if it is cooked in an air fryer.

Burning food is easy

The air fryer cooks food at very high temperatures very quickly. The air fryer is your friend if you don't have much time.

However, because it gets so hot so quickly, burning food is too easy.

Unlike a traditional grill or frying pan, which allows you to see your food, the air fryer is enclosed and almost always opaque. By the time you notice the smell, it will be too late.

Air Fryers are Small

We said in the "benefits" chapter that an air fryer is small and compact. For some people, this will be beneficial, but it also makes the air fryer inappropriate for larger events (such as family gatherings) or for use in the hospitality industry (for example, if you own a cafe).

How to clean an air fryer

The old saying goes, "cleanliness is next to godliness" whether you believe that to be true or not, it's always important to keep your cooking equipment clean.

Not only does this look nicer, but it's also more hygienic and energy efficient, as the air fryer only needs to heat up your food, not the grime.

If you fail to clean your air fryer, it will leave a nasty smell whenever you cook, and in some cases, it could even start smoking.

Our advice would be to clean it after every use. If you leave it for too long, the dirt will become caked on and more difficult to clean.

How to clean an air fryer (Method #1)

1. Unplug your air fryer, leave it to cool, and start by wiping it down to remove the worst of the grime.

Please note when I say "leave it to cool", I mean cool enough to touch, not cool enough for the dirt to solidify.

2. Use warm soapy water and a soft cloth to take off the bits of food and grease. The best type of soap to use is probably dish soap as it's designed to be tough and take off lots of fat.
3. If stains on the basket are too stubborn, remove the basket, and leave it to soak in warm soapy water for an hour or two.
4. Use a wooden skewer to get into the nooks and crannies you cannot get into with the soft cloth. You could also use a thin cleaning brush, which you can buy from places such as Dollar Tree or Poundland.
5. Use a damp cloth to degunk the inside of your air fryer.

How to clean an air fryer (Method #2)

There is another method, although I'm not sure how well this method works. I've tried it myself and can't figure out why it went wrong. But, I've heard other people who use the same process, say it works a treat.

I'll leave you to decide whether this method is legit or just clickbait.

1. Add dish soap and water into your air fryer.
2. Allow it to cook for 5 minutes at a medium temperature.
3. Pour out the hot soapy mixture. As you pour it out, the bits of food will pour out with it.
4. Rinse out the air fryer with plain water.
5. Dry with a tea towel or kitchen towel.

By the way, my advice about cleaning after use, not just when you notice a smell, applies to almost everything in your kitchen, not just the air fryer.

If you don't clean your air fryer, expect your food to take longer, bacteria to fester, and your kitchen to begin smoking.

Tips and Tricks

To finish this e-book, I've compiled a list of some tips and tricks I've learnt from using my air fryer.

Make sure the basket is always clean.

We spoke about this in the previous chapter. When your air fryer is clean, it will be more hygienic and efficient.

Don't wait for the dirt to solidify, clean it as soon as it gets dirty.

If you use parchment paper, also use heat-safe magnets

Some recipes may require you to preheat your air fryer with a layer of parchment paper. The problem is that the parchment paper can get blown around because of the fan. The solution is simply to use 4 heat-safe magnets to keep the paper attached to the device.

Place foil at the bottom for easy cleaning.
If you're cooking with more oil than usual, add a sheet of aluminium foil below the basket. Fat will drop onto the basket instead of the air fryer. Once the fat has cooled, you can remove it easily.

Par Boil your vegetables.
If you put raw vegetables such as carrots, swede, or potatoes into your air fryer, they will burn on the outside before they have cooked inside.
Therefore, we recommend boiling them in water for 5 minutes.

Start using your air fryer asap.
Some people are worried they'll make awful meals or want to read some more recipe books before starting. Our advice is to use your air fryer on day one.
The only way to learn is from your mistakes, and you need to use your air fryer to make mistakes.

Don't start with expensive stuff.
If you're new to the air fryer, maybe don't use lots of expensive ingredients. Use cheap vegetables or french fries.
Once you're confident with what you're doing, you can start to use more expensive ingredients.

Don't take times and temperatures as gospel.
Whenever you read a time and temperature in a recipe, remember that the chef's fryer will likely be different from your own.
If you notice your food always burns, use less time than the recipe calls for. If it's never done, use more time.
You could also adjust the temperature. Trial and error is better than treating recipes like gospel.
Also, open and check on your food. Most air fryers are designed to automatically turn off when they're opened.

General Advice
- Use a wireless thermometer to make sure meat like chicken is safe to eat.
- Never put your air fryer on the stove.
- Buy a reusable spray bottle and fill it with your preferred oil.
- Use foil to lift soft foods.

Chapter 1 Breakfasts

Peppe Spinach Omelet

Prep time: 5 minutes | Cook time: 12 minutes | Serves 2

INGREDIENTS

4 large eggs
2 tablespoons peeled and chopped yellow onion
60 g shredded mild Cheddar cheese
30 g chopped fresh spinach leaves
2 tablespoons salted butter, melted
¼ teaspoon salt

DIRECTIONS

1. In an ungreased round nonstick baking dish, whisk eggs. Stir in spinach, onion, butter, Cheddar, and salt.
2. Place dish into air fryer basket. Adjust the temperature to 160°C and bake for 12 minutes. Omelet will be done when browned on the top and firm in the middle.
3. Slice in half and serve warm on two medium plates.

Veggie Frittata

Prep time: 7 minutes | Cook time: 21 to 23 minutes | Serves 2

INGREDIENTS

Avocado oil spray
30 g diced red bell pepper
4 large eggs
½ teaspoon dried thyme
30 g diced red onion
30 g finely chopped broccoli
85 g shredded sharp Cheddar cheese, divided
Sea salt and freshly ground black pepper, to taste

DIRECTIONS

1. Spray a pan well with oil. Put the onion, pepper, and broccoli in the pan, place the pan in the air fryer, and set to 176°C. Bake for 5 minutes.
2. While the vegetables cook, beat the eggs in a medium bowl. Stir in half of the cheese, and season with the thyme, salt, and pepper.
3. Add the eggs to the pan and top with the remaining cheese. Set the air fryer to 176°C. Bake for 16 to 18 minutes, until cooked through.

Breakfast Pita

Prep time: 5 minutes | Cook time: 6 minutes | Serves 2

INGREDIENTS

1 whole wheat pita
¼ teaspoon garlic, minced
¼ teaspoon dried thyme
2 teaspoons olive oil
1 large egg
⅛ teaspoon salt
½ shallot, diced
¼ teaspoon dried oregano
2 tablespoons shredded Parmesan cheese

DIRECTIONS

1. Preheat the air fryer to 192°C.

2. Brush the top of the pita with olive oil, then spread the diced shallot and minced garlic over the pita.
3. Crack the egg into a small bowl or ramekin, and season it with oregano, thyme, and salt.
4. Place the pita into the air fryer basket, and gently pour the egg onto the top of the pita. Sprinkle with cheese over the top.
5. Bake for 6 minutes.
6. Allow to cool for 5 minutes before cutting into pieces for serving.

Cheesy Cauliflower "Hash Browns"

Prep time: 30 minutes | Cook time: 24 minutes | Makes 6 hash browns

INGREDIENTS

60 g 100% cheese crisps
1 large egg
1 (340 g) steam bag cauliflower, cooked according to package instructions
60 g shredded sharp Cheddar cheese
½ teaspoon salt

DIRECTIONS

1. Let cooked cauliflower cool 10 minutes.
2. Place cheese crisps into food processor and pulse on low 30 seconds until crisps are finely ground.
3. Using a kitchen towel, wring out excess moisture from cauliflower and place into food processor.
4. Add egg to food processor and sprinkle with Cheddar and salt. Pulse five times until mixture is mostly smooth.
5. Cut two pieces of baking paper to fit air fryer basket. Separate mixture into six even scoops and place three on each piece of ungreased baking paper, keeping at least 2 inch of space between each scoop. Press each into a hash brown shape, about ¼ inch thick.
6. Place one batch on baking paper into air fryer basket. Adjust the temperature to 192°C and air fry for 12 minutes, turning hash browns halfway through cooking. Hash browns will be golden brown when done. Repeat with second batch.
7. Allow 5 minutes to cool. Serve warm.

Gold Avocado

Prep time: 5 minutes | Cook time: 6 minutes | Serves 4

INGREDIENTS

2 large avocados, sliced
60 g plain flour
¼ teaspoon paprika
2 eggs, beaten
Salt and ground black pepper, to taste
125 g bread crumbs

DIRECTIONS

1. Preheat the air fryer to 204°C.
2. Sprinkle paprika, salt and pepper on the slices of avocado.
3. Lightly coat the avocados with flour. Dredge them in the eggs, before covering with bread crumbs.
4. Transfer to the air fryer and air fry for 6 minutes.
5. Serve warm.

Baked Peach Oatmeal

Prep time: 5 minutes | Cook time: 30 minutes | Serves 6

INGREDIENTS

Olive oil cooking spray

500 ml unsweetened almond milk

125 g nonfat plain Greek yogurt

½ teaspoon ground cinnamon

185 g diced peaches, divided, plus more for serving (optional)

250 g certified gluten-free rolled oats

60 g raw honey, plus more for drizzling (optional)

1 teaspoon vanilla extract

¼ teaspoon salt

DIRECTIONS

1. Preheat the air fryer to 192°C. Lightly coat the inside of a 6-inch cake pan with olive oil cooking spray.
2. In a large bowl, mix together the oats, almond milk, honey, yogurt, vanilla, cinnamon, and salt until well combined.
3. Fold in 95 g peaches and then pour the mixture into the prepared cake pan.
4. Sprinkle the remaining peaches across the top of the oatmeal mixture. Bake in the air fryer for 30 minutes.
5. Allow to set and cool for 5 minutes before serving with additional fresh fruit and honey for drizzling, if desired.

Bunless Breakfast Turkey Burgers

Prep time: 5 minutes | Cook time: 15 minutes | Serves 4

INGREDIENTS

455 g ground turkey sausage, skinned

¼ teaspoon ground black pepper

2 tablespoons mayonnaise

½ teaspoon salt

30 g seeded and chopped green bell pepper

1 medium avocado, peeled, pitted, and sliced

DIRECTIONS

1. In a large bowl, mix sausage with salt, black pepper, bell pepper, and mayonnaise. Form meat into four patties.
2. Place patties into ungreased air fryer basket. Adjust the temperature to 188°C and air fry for 15 minutes, turning patties halfway through cooking. Burgers will be done when dark brown and they have an internal temperature of at least 76°C.
3. Serve burgers topped with avocado slices on four medium plates.

Hole in One

Prep time: 5 minutes | Cook time: 6 to 7 minutes | Serves 1

INGREDIENTS

1 slice bread

Salt and pepper, to taste

1 teaspoon soft butter

1 tablespoon shredded Cheddar cheese

1 egg

2 teaspoons diced ham

DIRECTIONS

1. Place a baking dish inside air fryer basket and preheat the air fryer to 164°C.

2. Using a 2½-inch-diameter biscuit cutter, cut a hole in center of bread slice.
3. Spread softened butter on both sides of bread.
4. Lay bread slice in baking dish and crack egg into the hole. Sprinkle egg with salt and pepper to taste.
5. Cook for 5 minutes.
6. Turn toast over and top it with shredded cheese and diced ham.
7. Cook for 1 to 2 more minutes or until yolk is done to your liking.

Banana-Nut Muffins

Prep time: 5 minutes | Cook time: 15 minutes | Makes 10 muffins

INGREDIENTS

Oil, for spraying
80 ml rapeseed oil or vegetable oil
95 g plain flour
60 g chopped walnuts
2 very ripe bananas
1 large egg
1 teaspoon baking powder
60 g packed light brown sugar
1 teaspoon vanilla extract
1 teaspoon ground cinnamon

DIRECTIONS

1. Preheat the air fryer to 160°C. Spray 10 silicone muffin cups lightly with oil.
2. In a medium bowl, mash the bananas. Add the brown sugar, canola oil, egg, and vanilla and stir to combine.
3. Fold in the flour, baking powder, and cinnamon until just combined.
4. Add the walnuts and fold a few times to distribute throughout the batter.
5. Divide the batter equally among the prepared muffin cups and place them in the basket. You may need to work in batches, depending on the size of your air fryer.
6. Cook for 15 minutes, or until golden brown and a toothpick inserted into the center of a muffin comes out clean. The air fryer tends to brown muffins more than the oven, so don't be alarmed if they are darker than you're used to. They will still taste great.
7. Let cool on a wire rack before serving.

Breakfast Meatballs

Prep time: 10 minutes | Cook time: 15 minutes | Makes 18 meatballs

INGREDIENTS

455 g ground herbed pork sausage meat
¼ teaspoon ground black pepper
30 g cream cheese, softened
½ teaspoon salt
60 g shredded sharp Cheddar cheese
1 large egg, whisked

DIRECTIONS

1. Combine all ingredients in a large bowl. Form mixture into eighteen 1-inch meatballs.
2. Place meatballs into ungreased air fryer basket. Adjust the temperature to 204°C and air fry for 15 minutes, shaking basket three times during cooking. Meatballs will be browned on the outside and have an internal temperature of at least 64°C when completely cooked. Serve warm.

Sausage and Egg Breakfast Burrito

Prep time: 5 minutes | Cook time: 30 minutes | Serves 6

INGREDIENTS

6 eggs	Salt and pepper, to taste	Cooking oil
60 g chopped red bell pepper	60 g chopped green bell pepper	230 g ground chicken sausage
125 g salsa	6 medium (8-inch) flour tortillas	60 g shredded Cheddar cheese

DIRECTIONS

1. In a medium bowl, whisk the eggs. Add salt and pepper to taste.
2. Place a skillet on medium-high heat. Spray with cooking oil. Add the eggs. Scramble for 2 to 3 minutes, until the eggs are fluffy. Remove the eggs from the skillet and set aside.
3. If needed, spray the skillet with more oil. Add the chopped red and green bell peppers. Cook for 2 to 3 minutes, until the peppers are soft.
4. Add the ground sausage to the skillet. Break the sausage into smaller pieces using a spatula or spoon. Cook for 3 to 4 minutes, until the sausage is brown.
5. Add the salsa and scrambled eggs. Stir to combine. Remove the skillet from heat.
6. Spoon the mixture evenly onto the tortillas.
7. To form the burritos, fold the sides of each tortilla in toward the middle and then roll up from the bottom. You can secure each burrito with a toothpick. Or you can moisten the outside edge of the tortilla with a small amount of water. I prefer to use a cooking brush, but you can also dab with your fingers.
8. Spray the burritos with cooking oil and place them in the air fryer. Do not stack. Cook the burritos in batches if they do not all fit in the basket. Air fry at 204°C for 8 minutes.
9. Open the air fryer and flip the burritos. Cook for an additional 2 minutes or until crisp.
10. If necessary, repeat steps 8 and 9 for the remaining burritos.
11. Sprinkle the Cheddar cheese over the burritos. Cool before serving.

Broccoli-Mushroom Frittata

Prep time: 10 minutes | Cook time: 20 minutes | Serves 2

INGREDIENTS

1 tablespoon olive oil	185 g broccoli florets, finely chopped
60 g sliced brown mushrooms	30 g finely chopped onion
½ teaspoon salt	¼ teaspoon freshly ground black pepper
6 eggs	30 g Parmesan cheese

DIRECTIONS

1. In a nonstick cake pan, combine the olive oil, broccoli, mushrooms, onion, salt, and pepper. Stir until the vegetables are thoroughly coated with oil. Place the cake pan in the air fryer basket and set the air fryer to 204°C. Air fry for 5 minutes until the vegetables soften.
2. Meanwhile, in a medium bowl, whisk the eggs and Parmesan until thoroughly combined. Pour the egg mixture into the pan and shake gently to distribute the vegetables. Air fry for another 15 minutes until the eggs are set.

3. Remove from the air fryer and let sit for 5 minutes to cool slightly. Use a silicone spatula to gently lift the frittata onto a plate before serving.

Bacon Muffin Sandwiches

Prep time: 5 minutes | Cook time: 8 minutes | Serves 4

INGREDIENTS

4 English muffins, split
4 slices cheese
8 bacon medallions
Cooking spray

DIRECTIONS

1. Preheat the air fryer to 188°C.
2. Make the sandwiches: Top each of 4 muffin halves with 2 slices of Canadian bacon, 1 slice of cheese, and finish with the remaining muffin half.
3. Put the sandwiches in the air fryer basket and spritz the tops with cooking spray.
4. Bake for 4 minutes. Flip the sandwiches and bake for another 4 minutes.
5. Divide the sandwiches among four plates and serve warm.

Breakfast Calzone

Prep time: 15 minutes | Cook time: 15 minutes | Serves 4

INGREDIENTS

185 g shredded Mozzarella cheese
30 g full-fat cream cheese
4 large eggs, scrambled
8 tablespoons shredded mild Cheddar cheese
60 g blanched finely ground almond flour
1 large whole egg
230 g cooked sausage meat, crumbled

DIRECTIONS

1. In a large microwave-safe bowl, add Mozzarella, almond flour, and cream cheese. Microwave for 1 minute. Stir until the mixture is smooth and forms a ball. Add the egg and stir until dough forms.
2. Place dough between two sheets of baking paper and roll out to ¼-inch thickness. Cut the dough into four rectangles.
3. Mix scrambled eggs and cooked sausage together in a large bowl. Divide the mixture evenly among each piece of dough, placing it on the lower half of the rectangle. Sprinkle each with 2 tablespoons Cheddar.
4. Fold over the rectangle to cover the egg and meat mixture. Pinch, roll, or use a wet fork to close the edges completely.
5. Cut a piece of baking paper to fit your air fryer basket and place the calzones onto the baking paper. Place baking paper into the air fryer basket.
6. Adjust the temperature to 192°C and air fry for 15 minutes.
7. Flip the calzones halfway through the cooking time. When done, calzones should be golden in color. Serve immediately.

Creamy Cinnamon Rolls

Prep time: 10 minutes | Cook time: 9 minutes | Serves 8

INGREDIENTS

455 g frozen shortcrust pastry, thawed

95 g brown sugar

60 g butter, melted

1½ tablespoons ground cinnamon

Cream Cheese Glaze:

110 g cream cheese, softened

160 g powdered sugar

2 tablespoons butter, softened

½ teaspoon vanilla extract

DIRECTIONS

1. Let the bread dough come to room temperature on the counter. On a lightly floured surface, roll the dough into a 13-inch by 11-inch rectangle. Position the rectangle so the 13-inch side is facing you. Brush the melted butter all over the dough, leaving a 1-inch border uncovered along the edge farthest away from you.
2. Combine the brown sugar and cinnamon in a small bowl. Sprinkle the mixture evenly over the buttered dough, keeping the 1-inch border uncovered. Roll the dough into a log, starting with the edge closest to you. Roll the dough tightly, rolling evenly, and push out any air pockets. When you get to the uncovered edge of the dough, press the dough onto the roll to seal it together.
3. Cut the log into 8 pieces, slicing slowly with a sawing motion so you don't flatten the dough.
4. Turn the slices on their sides and cover with a clean kitchen towel. Let the rolls sit in the warmest part of the kitchen for 1½ to 2 hours to rise.
5. To make the glaze, place the cream cheese and butter in a microwave-safe bowl. Soften the mixture in the microwave for 30 seconds at a time until it is easy to stir. Gradually add the powdered sugar and stir to combine. Add the vanilla extract and whisk until smooth. Set aside.
6. When the rolls have risen, preheat the air fryer to 176ºC.
7. Transfer 4 of the rolls to the air fryer basket. Air fry for 5 minutes. Turn the rolls over and air fry for another 4 minutes. Repeat with the remaining 4 rolls.
8. Let the rolls cool for two minutes before glazing. Spread large dollops of cream cheese glaze on top of the warm cinnamon rolls, allowing some glaze to drip down the side of the rolls. Serve warm.

Mozzarella Bacon Calzones

Prep time: 15 minutes | Cook time: 12 minutes | Serves 4

INGREDIENTS

2 large eggs

250 g shredded Mozzarella cheese

4 slices cooked bacon, crumbled

125 g blanched finely ground almond flour

60 g cream cheese, softened and broken into small pieces

DIRECTIONS

1. Beat eggs in a small bowl. Pour into a medium nonstick skillet over medium heat and scramble. Set aside.
2. In a large microwave-safe bowl, mix flour and MozzarellAdd cream cheese to the bowl.
3. Place bowl in microwave and cook 45 seconds on high to melt cheese, then stir with a fork until a soft dough ball forms.

4. Cut a piece of baking paper to fit air fryer basket. Separate dough into two sections and press each out into an 8-inch round.

5. On half of each dough round, place half of the scrambled eggs and crumbled bacon. Fold the other side of the dough over and press to seal the edges.

6. Place calzones on ungreased baking paper and into air fryer basket. Adjust the temperature to 176°C and set the timer for 12 minutes, turning calzones halfway through cooking. Crust will be golden and firm when done.

7. Let calzones cool on a cooking rack 5 minutes before serving.

Chapter 2 Fish and seafood

New Orleans-Style Crab Cakes

Prep time: 10 minutes | Cook time: 8 to 10 minutes | Serves 4

INGREDIENTS

160 g bread crumbs
1 teaspoon salt
2 large eggs, beaten
Cooking spray
2 teaspoons Creole Seasoning
1 teaspoon freshly ground black pepper
1 teaspoon butter, melted
Pecan Tartar Sauce, for serving
1 teaspoon dry mustard
185 g crab meat
40 g minced onion

DIRECTIONS

1. Preheat the air fryer to 176°C. Line the air fryer basket with baking paper.
2. In a medium bowl, whisk the bread crumbs, Creole Seasoning, dry mustard, salt, and pepper until blended. Add the crab meat, eggs, butter, and onion. Stir until blended. Shape the crab mixture into 8 patties.
3. Place the crab cakes on the baking paper and spritz with oil.
4. Air fry for 4 minutes. Flip the cakes, spritz them with oil, and air fry for 4 to 6 minutes more until the outsides are firm and a fork inserted into the center comes out clean. Serve with the Pecan Tartar Sauce.

Apple Cider Mussels

Prep time: 10 minutes | Cook time: 2 minutes | Serves 5

INGREDIENTS

910 g mussels, cleaned and debearded
1 tablespoon avocado oil
1 teaspoon onion powder
65 ml apple cider vinegar
1 teaspoon ground cumin

DIRECTIONS

1. Mix mussels with onion powder, ground cumin, avocado oil, and apple cider vinegar.
2. Put the mussels in the air fryer and cook at 200°C for 2 minutes.

Crab-Stuffed Avocado Boats

Prep time: 5 minutes | Cook time: 7 minutes | Serves 4

INGREDIENTS

2 medium avocados, halved and pitted
¼ teaspoon Old Bay seasoning
2 tablespoons mayonnaise
230 g cooked crab meat
2 tablespoons peeled and diced yellow onion

DIRECTIONS

1. Scoop out avocado flesh in each avocado half, leaving ½ inch around edges to form a shell. Chop scooped-out avocado.
2. In a medium bowl, combine crab meat, Old Bay seasoning, onion, mayonnaise, and chopped avocado. Place ¼ mixture into each avocado shell.
3. Place avocado boats into ungreased air fryer basket. Adjust the temperature to 176°C and air fry for 7

minutes. Avocado will be browned on the top and mixture will be bubbling when done. Serve warm.

Tuna and Fruit Kebabs

Prep time: 15 minutes | Cook time: 8 to 12 minutes | Serves 4

INGREDIENTS

455 g tuna steaks, cut into 1-inch cubes
60 g canned pineapple chunks, drained, juice reserved
60 g large red grapes
1 tablespoon honey
2 teaspoons grated fresh ginger
1 teaspoon olive oil
Pinch cayenne pepper

DIRECTIONS

1. Thread the tuna, pineapple, and grapes on 8 bamboo or 4 metal skewers that fit in the air fryer.
2. In a small bowl, whisk the honey, 1 tablespoon of reserved pineapple juice, the ginger, olive oil, and cayenne. Brush this mixture over the kebabs. Let them stand for 10 minutes.
3. Air fry the kebabs at 188°C for 8 to 12 minutes, or until the tuna reaches an internal temperature of at least 64°C on a meat thermometer, and the fruit is tender and glazed, brushing once with the remaining sauce. Discard any remaining marinade. Serve immediately.

Southern-Style Catfish

Prep time: 10 minutes | Cook time: 12 minutes | Serves 4

INGREDIENTS

4 (200 g) catfish fillets
80 g heavy whipping cream
1 tablespoon lemon juice
125 g blanched finely ground almond flour
2 teaspoons Old Bay seasoning
½ teaspoon salt
¼ teaspoon ground black pepper

DIRECTIONS

1. Place catfish fillets into a large bowl with cream and pour in lemon juice. Stir to coat.
2. In a separate large bowl, mix flour and Old Bay seasoning.
3. Remove each fillet and gently shake off excess cream. Sprinkle with salt and pepper. Press each fillet gently into flour mixture on both sides to coat.
4. Place fillets into ungreased air fryer basket. Adjust the temperature to 204°C and air fry for 12 minutes, turning fillets halfway through cooking. Catfish will be golden brown and have an internal temperature of at least 64°C when done. Serve warm.

Smoky Prawn and Chorizo Tapas

Prep time: 15 minutes | Cook time: 10 minutes | Serves 2 to 4

INGREDIENTS

110 g Spanish (cured) chorizo, halved horizontally and sliced crosswise
230 g raw medium prawns, peeled and deveined
1 tablespoon extra-virgin olive oil
1 small shallot, halved and thinly sliced
1 garlic clove, minced
1 tablespoon finely chopped fresh oregano
½ teaspoon smoked Spanish paprika
¼ teaspoon kosher or coarse sea salt
¼ teaspoon black pepper
3 tablespoons fresh orange juice
1 tablespoon minced fresh parsley

DIRECTIONS

1. Place the chorizo in a baking pan. Set the pan in the air fryer basket. Set the air fryer to 192°C for 5 minutes, or until the chorizo has started to brown and render its fat.
2. Meanwhile, in a large bowl, combine the prawns, olive oil, shallot, garlic, oregano, paprika, salt, and pepper. Toss until the prawns are well coated.
3. Transfer the prawns to the pan with the chorizo. Stir to combine. Place the pan in the air fryer basket. Cook for 10 minutes, stirring halfway through the cooking time.
4. Transfer the prawns and chorizo to a serving dish. Drizzle with the orange juice and toss to combine. Sprinkle with the parsley.

Crab Legs

Prep time: 5 minutes | Cook time: 15 minutes | Serves 4

INGREDIENTS

60 g salted butter, melted and divided
¼ teaspoon garlic powder
1.4 kg crab legs
Juice of ½ medium lemon

DIRECTIONS

1. In a large bowl, drizzle 2 tablespoons butter over crab legs. Place crab legs into the air fryer basket.
2. Adjust the temperature to 204°C and air fry for 15 minutes.
3. Shake the air fryer basket to toss the crab legs halfway through the cooking time.
4. In a small bowl, mix remaining butter, garlic powder, and lemon juice.
5. To serve, crack open crab legs and remove meat. Dip in lemon butter.

Snapper Scampi

Prep time: 5 minutes | Cook time: 8 to 10 minutes | Serves 4

INGREDIENTS

4 (170 g) skinless snapper or arctic char fillets
3 tablespoons lemon juice, divided
Freshly ground black pepper, to taste
½ teaspoon dried basil
2 tablespoons butter
1 tablespoon olive oil
Pinch salt
2 cloves garlic, minced

DIRECTIONS

1. Rub the fish fillets with olive oil and 1 tablespoon of the lemon juice. Sprinkle with the basil, salt, and pepper, and place in the air fryer basket.
2. Air fry the fish at 192°C for 7 to 8 minutes or until the fish just flakes when tested with a fork. Remove the fish from the basket and put on a serving plate. Cover to keep warm.
3. In a baking pan, combine the butter, remaining 2 tablespoons lemon juice, and garlic. Bake in the air fryer for 1 to 2 minutes or until the garlic is sizzling. Pour this mixture over the fish and serve

Tilapia Sandwiches with Tartar Sauce

Prep time: 8 minutes | Cook time: 17 minutes | Serves 4

INGREDIENTS

185 g mayonnaise

1 dill pickle spear, finely chopped

¼ teaspoon salt

40 g plain flour

220 g panko bread crumbs

4 (170 g) tilapia fillets

4 soft subway rolls

2 tablespoons dried minced onion

2 teaspoons pickle juice

⅛ teaspoon freshly ground black pepper

1 egg, lightly beaten

2 teaspoons lemon pepper

Olive oil spray

4 butter lettuce leaves

DIRECTIONS

1. To make the tartar sauce, in a small bowl, whisk the mayonnaise, dried onion, pickle, pickle juice, salt, and pepper until blended. Refrigerate while you make the fish.
2. Scoop the flour onto a plate; set aside.
3. Put the beaten egg in a medium shallow bowl.
4. On another plate, stir together the panko and lemon pepper.
5. Insert the crisper plate into the basket and the basket into the unit. Preheat the unit by selecting AIR FRY, setting the temperature to 204ºC, and setting the time to 3 minutes. Select START/STOP to begin.
6. Dredge the tilapia fillets in the flour, in the egg, and press into the panko mixture to coat.
7. Once the unit is preheated, spray the crisper plate with olive oil and place a baking paper liner into the basket. Place the prepared fillets on the liner in a single layer. Lightly spray the fillets with olive oil.
8. Select AIR FRY, set the temperature to 204ºC, and set the time to 17 minutes. Select START/STOP to begin.
9. After 8 minutes, remove the basket, carefully flip the fillets, and spray them with more olive oil. Reinsert the basket to resume cooking.
10. When the cooking is complete, the fillets should be golden and crispy and a food thermometer should register 64ºC. Place each cooked fillet in a subway roll, top with a little bit of tartar sauce and lettuce, and serve.

Oregano Tilapia Fingers

Prep time: 15 minutes | Cook time: 9 minutes | Serves 4

INGREDIENTS

455 g tilapia fillet

½ teaspoon ground paprika

60 g coconut flour

1 teaspoon dried oregano

2 eggs, beaten

1 teaspoon avocado oil

DIRECTIONS

1. Cut the tilapia fillets into fingers and sprinkle with ground paprika and dried oregano.
2. Then dip the tilapia fingers in eggs and coat in the coconut flour.
3. Sprinkle fish fingers with avocado oil and cook in the air fryer at 188ºC for 9 minutes.

Almond-Crusted Fish

Prep time: 15 minutes | Cook time: 10 minutes | Serves 4

INGREDIENTS

4 (110 g) fish fillets
2 tablespoons lemon juice
95 g flour
Oil for misting or cooking spray
95 g bread crumbs
⅛ teaspoon cayenne
1 egg, beaten with 1 tablespoon water
30 g sliced almonds, crushed
Salt and pepper, to taste

DIRECTIONS

1. Split fish fillets lengthwise down the center to create 8 pieces.
2. Mix bread crumbs and almonds together and set aside.
3. Mix the lemon juice and cayenne together. Brush on all sides of fish.
4. Season fish to taste with salt and pepper.
5. Place the flour on a sheet of wax paper.
6. Roll fillets in flour, dip in egg wash, and roll in the crumb mixture.
7. Mist both sides of fish with oil or cooking spray.
8. Spray the air fryer basket and lay fillets inside.
9. Roast at 200°C for 5 minutes, turn fish over, and cook for an additional 5 minutes or until fish is done and flakes easily.

Marinated Salmon Fillets

Prep time: 10 minutes | Cook time: 15 to 20 minutes | Serves 4

INGREDIENTS

60 g soy sauce
1 tablespoon olive oil
½ teaspoon freshly ground black pepper
4 (170 g) salmon fillets, skin-on
65 ml rice wine vinegar
1 teaspoon mustard powder
½ teaspoon minced garlic
Cooking spray
1 tablespoon brown sugar
1 teaspoon ground ginger

DIRECTIONS

1. In a small bowl, combine the soy sauce, rice wine vinegar, brown sugar, olive oil, mustard powder, ginger, black pepper, and garlic to make a marinade.
2. Place the fillets in a shallow baking dish and pour the marinade over them. Cover the baking dish and marinate for at least 1 hour in the refrigerator, turning the fillets occasionally to keep them coated in the marinade.
3. Preheat the air fryer to 188°C. Spray the air fryer basket lightly with cooking spray.
4. Shake off as much marinade as possible from the fillets and place them, skin-side down, in the air fryer basket in a single layer. You may need to cook the fillets in batches.
5. Air fry for 15 to 20 minutes for well done. The minimum internal temperature should be 64°C at the thickest part of the fillets.
6. Serve hot.

Sweet Tilapia Fillets

Prep time: 5 minutes | Cook time: 14 minutes | Serves 4

INGREDIENTS

2 tablespoons granulated sweetener
1 tablespoon apple cider vinegar
4 tilapia fillets, boneless
1 teaspoon olive oil

DIRECTIONS

1. Mix apple cider vinegar with olive oil and sweetener.
2. Then rub the tilapia fillets with the sweet mixture and put in the air fryer basket in one layer. Cook the fish at 184°C for 7 minutes per side.

Chapter 3 Poultry

Fried Chicken Breasts

Prep time: 30 minutes | Cook time: 12 to 14 minutes | Serves 4

INGREDIENTS

450 g boneless, skinless chicken breasts
95 g finely ground blanched almond flour
½ teaspoon sea salt
2 large eggs
190 ml dill pickle juice
95 g finely grated Parmesan cheese
½ teaspoon freshly ground black pepper
Avocado oil spray

DIRECTIONS

1. Place the chicken breasts in a sandwich bag or between two pieces of cling film. Using a meat mallet or heavy skillet, pound the chicken to a uniform ½-inch thickness.
2. Place the chicken in a large bowl with the pickle juice. Cover and allow to brine in the refrigerator for up to 2 hours.
3. In a shallow dish, combine the almond flour, Parmesan cheese, salt, and pepper. In a separate, shallow bowl, beat the eggs.
4. Drain the chicken and pat it dry with paper towels. Dip in the eggs and then in the flour mixture, making sure to press the coating into the chicken. Spray both sides of the coated breasts with oil.
5. Spray the air fryer basket with oil and put the chicken inside. Set the temperature to 204ºC and air fry for 6 to 7 minutes.
6. Carefully flip the breasts with a spatula. Spray the breasts again with oil and continue cooking for 6 to 7 minutes more, until golden and crispy.

Chicken Schnitzel Dogs

Prep time: 15 minutes | Cook time: 8 to 10 minutes | Serves 4

INGREDIENTS

60 g plain flour
1 teaspoon dried parsley flakes
1 teaspoon lemon juice
4 chicken breast fillets, pounded thin
4 whole grain hotdog buns
1 small Granny Smith apple, thinly sliced
Coleslaw dressing
½ teaspoon salt
½ teaspoon thyme
1 teaspoon water
1 teaspoon marjoram
1 egg
125 g bread crumbs
Oil for misting or cooking spray
4 slices Gouda cheese
60 g shredded Savoy cabbage

DIRECTIONS

1. In a shallow dish, mix together the flour, salt, marjoram, parsley, and thyme.
2. In another shallow dish, beat together egg, lemon juice, and water.
3. Place bread crumbs in a third shallow dish.
4. Cut each of the flattened chicken fillets in half lengthwise.
5. Dip flattened chicken strips in flour mixture, then egg wash. Let excess egg drip off and roll in bread crumbs. Spray both sides with oil or cooking spray.

6. Air fry at 200ºC for 5 minutes. Spray with oil, turn over, and spray other side.
7. Cook for 3 to 5 minutes more, until well done and crispy brown.
8. To serve, place 2 schnitzel strips on bottom of each hotdog bun. Top with cheese, sliced apple, and cabbage. Drizzle with coleslaw dressing and top with other half of bun.

Chicken Breasts with Asparagus, Beans, and Rocket

Prep time: 20 minutes | Cook time: 25 minutes | Serves 2

INGREDIENTS

125 g canned cannellini beans, rinsed
1 garlic clove, minced
Salt and ground black pepper, to taste
230 g asparagus, trimmed and cut into 1-inch lengths
2 (230 g) boneless, skinless chicken breasts, trimmed
¼ teaspoon paprika
½ teaspoon ground coriander
1½ tablespoons red wine vinegar
2 tablespoons extra-virgin olive oil, divided
½ red onion, sliced thinly
60 g baby rocket, rinsed and drained

DIRECTIONS

1. Preheat the air fryer to 204ºC.
2. Warm the beans in microwave for 1 minutes and combine with red wine vinegar, garlic, 1 tablespoon of olive oil, ¼ teaspoon of salt, and ¼ teaspoon of ground black pepper in a bowl. Stir to mix well.
3. Combine the onion with ⅛ teaspoon of salt, ⅛ teaspoon of ground black pepper, and 2 teaspoons of olive oil in a separate bowl. Toss to coat well.
4. Place the onion in the air fryer and air fry for 2 minutes, then add the asparagus and air fry for 8 more minutes or until the asparagus is tender. Shake the basket halfway through. Transfer the onion and asparagus to the bowl with beans. Set aside.
5. Toss the chicken breasts with remaining ingredients, except for the baby arugula, in a large bowl.
6. Put the chicken breasts in the air fryer and air fry for 14 minutes or until the internal temperature of the chicken reaches at least 76ºC. Flip the breasts halfway through.
7. Remove the chicken from the air fryer and serve on an aluminum foil with asparagus, beans, onion, and rocket. Sprinkle with salt and ground black pepper. Toss to serve.

Crisp Paprika Chicken Drumsticks

Prep time: 5 minutes | Cook time: 22 minutes | Serves 2

INGREDIENTS

2 teaspoons paprika
½ teaspoon dry mustard
4 (140 g) chicken drumsticks, trimmed
1 spring onion, green part only, sliced thin on bias
1 teaspoon packed brown sugar
½ teaspoon salt
1 teaspoon garlic powder
Pinch pepper
1 teaspoon vegetable oil

DIRECTIONS

1. Preheat the air fryer to 204ºC.
2. Combine paprika, sugar, garlic powder, mustard, salt, and pepper in a bowl. Pat drumsticks dry with paper towels. Using metal skewer, poke 10 to 15 holes in skin of each drumstick. Rub with oil

and sprinkle evenly with spice mixture.

3. Arrange drumsticks in air fryer basket, spaced evenly apart, alternating ends. Air fry until chicken is crisp and registers 92°C, 22 to 25 minutes, flipping chicken halfway through cooking.

4. Transfer chicken to serving platter, tent loosely with aluminum foil, and let rest for 5 minutes. Sprinkle with spring onion and serve.

Thai-Style Cornish Game Hens

Prep time: 30 minutes | Cook time: 20 minutes | Serves 4

INGREDIENTS

20 g chopped fresh coriander leaves and stems
1 tablespoon soy sauce
8 garlic cloves, smashed
2 tablespoons lemongrass paste
2 teaspoons ground coriander
1 teaspoon ground turmeric
60 g fish sauce
1 Serrano chilli, seeded and chopped
2 tablespoons sugar
2 teaspoons black pepper
1 teaspoon kosher or coarse sea salt
2 Cornish game hens, giblets removed, split in half lengthwise

DIRECTIONS

1. In a blender, combine the coriander, fish sauce, soy sauce, Serrano, garlic, sugar, lemongrass, black pepper, coriander, salt, and turmeric. Blend until smooth.

2. Place the game hen halves in a large bowl. Pour the cilantro mixture over the hen halves and toss to coat. Marinate at room temperature for 30 minutes, or cover and refrigerate for up to 24 hours.

3. Arrange the hen halves in a single layer in the air fryer basket. Set the air fryer to 204°C for 20 minutes. Use a meat thermometer to ensure the game hens have reached an internal temperature of 76°C.

Smoky Chicken Leg Quarters

Prep time: 30 minutes | Cook time: 23 to 27 minutes | Serves 6

INGREDIENTS

125 ml avocado oil
1 teaspoon garlic powder
½ teaspoon freshly ground black pepper
2 teaspoons smoked paprika
½ teaspoon dried rosemary
1 teaspoon sea salt
½ teaspoon dried thyme
910 g bone-in, skin-on chicken leg quarters

DIRECTIONS

1. In a blender or small bowl, combine the avocado oil, smoked paprika, salt, garlic powder, rosemary, thyme, and black pepper.

2. Place the chicken in a shallow dish or large sandwich bag. Pour the marinade over the chicken, making sure all the legs are coated. Cover and marinate for at least 2 hours or overnight.

3. Place the chicken in a single layer in the air fryer basket, working in batches if necessary. Set the air fryer to 204°C and air fry for 15 minutes. Flip the chicken legs, then reduce the temperature to 176°C. Cook for 8 to 12 minutes more, until an instant-read thermometer reads 72°C when inserted into the thickest piece of chicken.

4. Allow to rest for 5 to 10 minutes before serving.

Golden Chicken Cutlets

Prep time: 15 minutes | Cook time: 15 minutes | Serves 4

INGREDIENTS

2 tablespoons panko breadcrumbs
½ tablespoon garlic powder
1 tablespoon parsley

30 g grated Parmesan cheese
2 large eggs
Salt and ground black pepper, to taste

⅛ tablespoon paprika
4 chicken cutlets
Cooking spray

DIRECTIONS

1. Preheat air fryer to 204°C. Spritz the air fryer basket with cooking spray.
2. Combine the breadcrumbs, Parmesan, paprika, garlic powder, salt, and ground black pepper in a large bowl. Stir to mix well. Beat the eggs in a separate bowl.
3. Dredge the chicken cutlets in the beaten eggs, then roll over the breadcrumbs mixture to coat well. Shake the excess off.
4. Transfer the chicken cutlets in the preheated air fryer and spritz with cooking spray.
5. Air fry for 15 minutes or until crispy and golden brown. Flip the cutlets halfway through.
6. Serve with parsley on top.

Pork Scratching Fried Chicken

Prep time: 30 minutes | Cook time: 20 minutes | Serves 4

INGREDIENTS

60 g buffalo sauce
½ teaspoon paprika
¼ teaspoon ground black pepper

4 (110 g) boneless, skinless chicken breasts
½ teaspoon garlic powder
60 g pork scratchings, finely crushed

DIRECTIONS

1. Pour buffalo sauce into a large sealable bowl or bag. Add chicken and toss to coat. Place sealed bowl or bag into refrigerator and let marinate at least 30 minutes up to overnight.
2. Remove chicken from marinade but do not shake excess sauce off chicken. Sprinkle both sides of thighs with paprika, garlic powder, and pepper.
3. Place pork scratchings into a large bowl and press each chicken breast into scratchings to coat evenly on both sides.
4. Place chicken into ungreased air fryer basket. Adjust the temperature to 204°C and roast for 20 minutes, turning chicken halfway through cooking. Chicken will be golden and have an internal temperature of at least 76°C when done. Serve warm.

Bacon Lovers' Stuffed Chicken

Prep time: 10 minutes | Cook time: 20 minutes | Serves 4

INGREDIENTS

4 (140 g) boneless, skinless chicken breasts, pounded to ¼ inch thick
2 (150 g) packages Boursin cheese (or Kite Hill brand chive cream cheese style spread, softened, for dairy-free)
8 slices thin-cut bacon
Sprig of fresh coriander, for garnish (optional)

DIRECTIONS

1. Spray the air fryer basket with avocado oil. Preheat the air fryer to 204°C.
2. Place one of the chicken breasts on a cutting board. With a sharp knife held parallel to the cutting board, make a 1-inch-wide incision at the top of the breast. Carefully cut into the breast to form a large pocket, leaving a ½-inch border along the sides and bottom. Repeat with the other 3 chicken breasts.
3. Snip the corner of a large sandwich bag to form a ¾-inch hole. Place the Boursin cheese in the bag and pipe the cheese into the pockets in the chicken breasts, dividing the cheese evenly among them.
4. Wrap 2 slices of bacon around each chicken breast and secure the ends with toothpicks. Place the bacon-wrapped chicken in the air fryer basket and air fry until the bacon is crisp and the chicken's internal temperature reaches 76°C, about 18 to 20 minutes, flipping after 10 minutes. Garnish with a sprig of coriander before serving, if desired.
5. Store leftovers in an airtight container in the refrigerator for up to 4 days. Reheat in a preheated 204°C air fryer for 5 minutes, or until warmed through.

'Bacon-Wrapped Stuffed Chicken Breasts

Prep time: 15 minutes | Cook time: 30 minutes | Serves 4

INGREDIENTS

10 g chopped frozen spinach, thawed and squeezed dry
30 g grated Parmesan cheese
½ teaspoon kosher or coarse sea salt
2 large boneless, skinless chicken breasts, butterflied and pounded to ½-inch thickness
4 teaspoons salt-free Cajun seasoning
30 g cream cheese, softened
1 jalapeño, seeded and chopped
1 teaspoon black pepper
6 slices bacon

DIRECTIONS

1. In a small bowl, combine the spinach, cream cheese, Parmesan cheese, jalapeño, salt, and pepper. Stir until well combined.
2. Place the butterflied chicken breasts on a flat surface. Spread the cream cheese mixture evenly across each piece of chicken. Starting with the narrow end, roll up each chicken breast, ensuring the filling stays inside. Season chicken with the Cajun seasoning, patting it in to ensure it sticks to the meat.
3. Wrap each breast in 3 slices of bacon. Place in the air fryer basket. Set the air fryer to 176°C for 30 minutes. Use a meat thermometer to ensure the chicken has reached an internal temperature of 76°C.
4. Let the chicken stand 5 minutes before slicing each rolled-up breast in half to serve.

Chapter 4 Vegetables and Sides

Green Tomato Salad

Prep time: 10 minutes | Cook time: 8 to 10 minutes | Serves 4

INGREDIENTS

4 green tomatoes
60 g peanut flour
½ teaspoon salt
1 tablespoon Creole seasoning
1 large egg, lightly beaten
1 (140 g) bag rocket

Buttermilk Dressing:

250 g mayonnaise
2 tablespoons finely chopped fresh parsley
1 teaspoon dried chives
½ teaspoon onion powder
125 g sour cream
½ teaspoon salt
2 teaspoons fresh lemon juice
1 teaspoon dried dill
½ teaspoon garlic powder

DIRECTIONS

1. Preheat the air fryer to 204°C.
2. Slice the tomatoes into ½-inch slices and sprinkle with the salt. Let sit for 5 to 10 minutes.
3. Place the egg in a small shallow bowl. In another small shallow bowl, combine the peanut flour and Creole seasoning. Dip each tomato slice into the egg wash, then dip into the peanut flour mixture, turning to coat evenly.
4. Working in batches if necessary, arrange the tomato slices in a single layer in the air fryer basket and spray both sides lightly with olive oil. Air fry until browned and crisp, 8 to 10 minutes.
5. To make the buttermilk dressing: In a small bowl, whisk together the mayonnaise, sour cream, lemon juice, parsley, dill, chives, salt, garlic powder, and onion powder.
6. Serve the tomato slices on top of a bed of the arugula with the dressing on the side.

Kohlrabi Fries

Prep time: 10 minutes | Cook time: 20 to 30 minutes | Serves 4

INGREDIENTS

910 g kohlrabi, peeled and cut into ¼ to ½-inch fries
2 tablespoons olive oil
Salt and freshly ground black pepper, to taste

DIRECTIONS

1. Preheat the air fryer to 204°C.
2. In a large bowl, combine the kohlrabi and olive oil. Season to taste with salt and black pepper. Toss gently until thoroughly coated.
3. Working in batches if necessary, spread the kohlrabi in a single layer in the air fryer basket. Pausing halfway through the cooking time to shake the basket, air fry for 20 to 30 minutes until the fries are lightly browned and crunchy.

Curried Fruit

Prep time: 10 minutes | Cook time: 20 minutes | Serves 6 to 8

INGREDIENTS

125 g cubed fresh pineapple

230 g frozen peaches, thawed

2 tablespoons brown sugar

125 g cubed fresh pear (firm, not overly ripe)

1 (425 g) can dark, sweet, pitted cherries with juice

1 teaspoon curry powder

DIRECTIONS

1. Combine all ingredients in large bowl. Stir gently to mix in the sugar and curry.
2. Pour into a baking pan and bake at 184°C for 10 minutes.
3. Stir fruit and cook 10 more minutes.
4. Serve hot.

Hasselback Potatoes with Chive Pesto

Prep time: 10 minutes | Cook time: 40 minutes | Serves 2

INGREDIENTS

2 medium russet potatoes

5 tablespoons olive oil

Kosher or coarse sea salt and freshly ground black pepper, to taste

5 g roughly chopped fresh chives

2 tablespoons packed fresh flat-leaf parsley leaves

1 tablespoon chopped walnuts

1 tablespoon grated Parmesan cheese

1 teaspoon fresh lemon juice

1 small garlic clove, peeled

60 g sour cream

DIRECTIONS

1. Place the potatoes on a cutting board and lay a chopstick or thin-handled wooden spoon to the side of each potato. Thinly slice the potatoes crosswise, letting the chopstick or spoon handle stop the blade of your knife, and stop ½ inch short of each end of the potato. Rub the potatoes with 1 tablespoon of the olive oil and season with salt and pepper.
2. Place the potatoes, cut-side up, in the air fryer and air fry at 192°C until golden brown and crisp on the outside and tender inside, about 40 minutes, drizzling the insides with 1 tablespoon more olive oil and seasoning with more salt and pepper halfway through.
3. Meanwhile, in a small blender or food processor, combine the remaining 3 tablespoons olive oil, the chives, parsley, walnuts, Parmesan, lemon juice, and garlic and purée until smooth. Season the chive pesto with salt and pepper.
4. Remove the potatoes from the air fryer and transfer to plates. Drizzle the potatoes with the pesto, letting it drip down into the grooves, then dollop each with sour cream and serve hot.

Asparagus Fries

Prep time: 15 minutes | Cook time: 5 to 7 minutes per batch | Serves 4

INGREDIENTS

340 g fresh asparagus spears with tough ends trimmed off
2 egg whites
60 ml water
95 g Panko bread crumbs
60 g grated Parmesan cheese, plus 2 tablespoons
¼ teaspoon salt
Oil for misting or cooking spray

DIRECTIONS

1. Preheat the air fryer to 200ºC.
2. In a shallow dish, beat egg whites and water until slightly foamy.
3. In another shallow dish, combine panko, Parmesan, and salt.
4. Dip asparagus spears in egg, then roll in crumbs. Spray with oil or cooking spray.
5. Place a layer of asparagus in air fryer basket, leaving just a little space in between each spear. Stack another layer on top, crosswise. Air fry at 200ºC for 5 to 7 minutes, until crispy and golden brown.
6. Repeat to cook remaining asparagus.

Indian Aubergine Bharta

Prep time: 15 minutes | Cook time: 20 minutes | Serves 4

INGREDIENTS

1 medium aubergine
2 tablespoons vegetable oil
60 g finely minced onion
60 g finely chopped fresh tomato
2 tablespoons fresh lemon juice
2 tablespoons chopped fresh coriander
½ teaspoon kosher or coarse salt
⅛ teaspoon cayenne pepper

DIRECTIONS

1. Rub the aubergine all over with the vegetable oil. Place the aubergine in the air fryer basket. Set the air fryer to 204ºC for 20 minutes, or until the aubergine skin is blistered and charred.
2. Transfer the aubergine to a large sandwich bag, seal, and set aside for 15 to 20 minutes (the aubergine will finish cooking in the residual heat trapped in the bag).
3. Transfer the aubergine to a large bowl. Peel off and discard the charred skin. Roughly mash the aubergine flesh. Add the onion, tomato, lemon juice, coriander, salt, and cayenne. Stir to combine.

Spiced Butternut Squash

Prep time: 10 minutes | Cook time: 15 minutes | Serves 4

INGREDIENTS

500 g 1-inch-cubed butternut squash
2 tablespoons vegetable oil
1 to 2 tablespoons brown sugar
1 teaspoon Chinese five-spice powder

DIRECTIONS

1. In a medium bowl, combine the squash, oil, sugar, and five-spice powder. Toss to coat.
2. Place the squash in the air fryer basket. Set the air fryer to 204ºC for 15 minutes or until tender.

Roasted Brussels Sprouts with Bacon

Prep time: 10 minutes | Cook time: 20 minutes | Serves 4

INGREDIENTS

4 slices thick-cut bacon, chopped (about 115 g)
450 g Brussels sprouts, halved (or quartered if large)
Freshly ground black pepper, to taste

DIRECTIONS

1. Preheat the air fryer to 192°C.
2. Air fry the bacon for 5 minutes, shaking the basket once or twice during the cooking time.
3. Add the Brussels sprouts to the basket and drizzle a little bacon fat from the bottom of the air fryer drawer into the basket. Toss the sprouts to coat with the bacon fat. Air fry for an additional 15 minutes, or until the Brussels sprouts are tender to a knifepoint.
4. Season with freshly ground black pepper.

Roasted Sweet Potatoes

Prep time: 10 minutes | Cook time: 25 minutes | Serves 4

INGREDIENTS

Cooking oil spray
1 tablespoon extra-virgin olive oil
Freshly ground black pepper, to taste
½ teaspoon dried marjoram
2 sweet potatoes, peeled and cut into 1-inch cubes
Pinch salt
½ teaspoon dried thyme
30 g grated Parmesan cheese

DIRECTIONS

1. Insert the crisper plate into the basket and the basket into the unit. Preheat the unit by selecting AIR ROAST, setting the temperature to 164°C, and setting the time to 3 minutes. Select START/STOP to begin.
2. Once the unit is preheated, spray the crisper plate with cooking oil. Put the sweet potato cubes into the basket and drizzle with olive oil. Toss gently to coat. Sprinkle with the salt, pepper, thyme, and marjoram and toss again.
3. Select AIR ROAST, set the temperature to 164°C, and set the time to 25 minutes. Select START/STOP to begin.
4. After 10 minutes, remove the basket and shake the potatoes. Reinsert the basket to resume cooking. After another 10 minutes, remove the basket and shake the potatoes one more time. Sprinkle evenly with the Parmesan cheese. Reinsert the basket to resume cooking.
5. When the cooking is complete, the potatoes should be tender. Serve immediately.

Radish Chips

Prep time: 10 minutes | Cook time: 5 minutes | Serves 4

INGREDIENTS

500 ml water
¼ teaspoon paprika
455 g radishes
½ teaspoon garlic powder
¼ teaspoon onion powder
2 tablespoons coconut oil, melted

DIRECTIONS

1. Place water in a medium saucepan and bring to a boil on stovetop.
2. Remove the top and bottom from each radish, then use a mandoline to slice each radish thin and uniformly. You may also use the slicing blade in the food processor for this step.
3. Place the radish slices into the boiling water for 5 minutes or until translucent. Remove them from the water and place them into a clean kitchen towel to absorb excess moisture.
4. Toss the radish chips in a large bowl with remaining ingredients until fully coated in oil and seasoning. Place radish chips into the air fryer basket.
5. Adjust the temperature to 160°C and air fry for 5 minutes.
6. Shake the basket two or three times during the cooking time. Serve warm.

Mashed Sweet Potato Tots

Prep time: 10 minutes | Cook time: 12 to 13 minutes per batch | Makes 18 to 24 tots

INGREDIENTS

125 g cooked mashed sweet potatoes
1 egg white, beaten
⅛ teaspoon ground cinnamon
1 dash nutmeg
2 tablespoons chopped pecans
1½ teaspoons honey
Salt, to taste
60 g panko bread crumbs
Oil for misting or cooking spray

DIRECTIONS

1. Preheat the air fryer to 200°C.
2. In a large bowl, mix together the potatoes, egg white, cinnamon, nutmeg, pecans, honey, and salt to taste.
3. Place panko crumbs on a sheet of wax paper.
4. For each tot, use about 2 teaspoons of sweet potato mixture. To shape, drop the measure of potato mixture onto panko crumbs and push crumbs up and around potatoes to coat edges. Then turn tot over to coat other side with crumbs.
5. Mist tots with oil or cooking spray and place in air fryer basket in single layer.
6. Air fry at 200°C for 12 to 13 minutes, until browned and crispy.
7. Repeat steps 5 and 6 to cook remaining tots.

Parsnip Fries with Romesco Sauce

Prep time: 20 minutes | Cook time: 24 minutes | Serves 4

INGREDIENTS

Romesco Sauce:

1 red bell pepper, halved and seeded
1 (1-inch) thick slice of Italian bread, torn into pieces
125 g almonds, toasted
Olive oil
½ Jalapeño pepper, seeded
1 tablespoon fresh parsley leaves
1 clove garlic
2 plum tomatoes, peeled and seeded (or 40 g canned crushed tomatoes)
1 tablespoon red wine vinegar
¼ teaspoon smoked paprika
½ teaspoon salt
185 ml olive oil
3 parsnips, peeled and cut into long strips
2 teaspoons olive oil
Salt and freshly ground black pepper, to taste

DIRECTIONS

1. Preheat the air fryer to 204°C.

2. Place the red pepper halves, cut side down, in the air fryer basket and air fry for 8 to 10 minutes, or until the skin turns black all over. Remove the pepper from the air fryer and let it cool. When it is cool enough to handle, peel the pepper.

3. Toss the torn bread and almonds with a little olive oil and air fry for 4 minutes, shaking the basket a couple times throughout the cooking time. When the bread and almonds are nicely toasted, remove them from the air fryer and let them cool for just a minute or two.

4. Combine the toasted bread, almonds, roasted red pepper, Jalapeño pepper, parsley, garlic, tomatoes, vinegar, smoked paprika and salt in a food processor or blender. Process until smooth. With the processor running, add the olive oil through the feed tube until the sauce comes together in a smooth paste that is barely pourable.

5. Toss the parsnip strips with the olive oil, salt and freshly ground black pepper and air fry at 204°C for 10 minutes, shaking the basket a couple times during the cooking process so they brown and cook evenly. Serve the parsnip fries warm with the Romesco sauce to dip into.

Garlic-Parmesan Crispy Baby Potatoes

Prep time: 10 minutes | Cook time: 15 minutes | Serves 4

INGREDIENTS

Oil, for spraying
3 tablespoons olive oil
½ teaspoon salt
¼ teaspoon paprika
455 g baby potatoes
2 teaspoons garlic granules
60 g grated Parmesan cheese, divided
½ teaspoon onion powder
¼ teaspoon freshly ground black pepper
2 tablespoons chopped fresh parsley, for garnish

DIRECTIONS

1. Line the air fryer basket with baking paper and spray lightly with oil.
2. Rinse the potatoes, pat dry with paper towels, and place in a large bowl.
3. In a small bowl, mix together 30 g Parmesan cheese, the olive oil, garlic, onion powder, salt, black pepper, and paprikPour the mixture over the potatoes and toss to coat.
4. Transfer the potatoes to the prepared basket and spread them out in an even layer, taking care to keep them from touching. You may need to work in batches, depending on the size of your air fryer.
5. Air fry at 204°C for 15 minutes, stirring after 7 to 8 minutes, or until easily pierced with a fork. Continue to cook for another 1 to 2 minutes, if needed.
6. Sprinkle with the parsley and the remaining Parmesan cheese and serve.

Garlic Roasted Broccoli

Prep time: 8 minutes | Cook time: 10 to 14 minutes | Serves 6

INGREDIENTS

1 head broccoli, cut into bite-sized florets
2 teaspoons minced garlic
Sea salt and freshly ground black pepper, to taste
½ teaspoon lemon zest
1 tablespoon avocado oil
⅛ teaspoon red pepper flakes
1 tablespoon freshly squeezed lemon juice

DIRECTIONS

1. In a large bowl, toss together the broccoli, avocado oil, garlic, red pepper flakes, salt, and pepper.

2. Set the air fryer to 192ºC. Arrange the broccoli in a single layer in the air fryer basket, working in batches if necessary. Roast for 10 to 14 minutes, until the broccoli is lightly charred.

3. Place the florets in a medium bowl and toss with the lemon juice and lemon zest. Serve.

Chermoula-Roasted Beets

Prep time: 15 minutes | Cook time: 25 minutes | Serves 4

INGREDIENTS

Chermoula:

20 g packed fresh coriander leaves

6 cloves garlic, peeled

2 teaspoons ground cumin

½ to 1 teaspoon cayenne pepper

125 ml extra-virgin olive oil

10 g packed fresh parsley leaves

2 teaspoons smoked paprika

1 teaspoon ground coriander

Pinch crushed saffron (optional)

Kosher or coarse sea salt, to taste

Beets:

3 medium beetroot, trimmed, peeled, and cut into 1-inch chunks

2 tablespoons chopped fresh coriander

2 tablespoons chopped fresh parsley

DIRECTIONS

1. For the chermoula: In a food processor, combine the coriander leaves, parsley, garlic, paprika, cumin, coriander, and cayenne. Pulse until coarsely chopped. Add the saffron, if using, and process until combined. With the food processor running, slowly add the olive oil in a steady stream; process until the sauce is uniform. Season to taste with salt.

2. For the beets: In a large bowl, drizzle the beetroot with 125 g the chermoula, or enough to coat. Arrange the beetroot in the air fryer basket. Set the air fryer to 192ºC for 25 to minutes, or until the beetroot is tender.

3. Transfer the beetroot to a serving platter. Sprinkle with chopped coriander and parsley and serve.

Chapter 5 Beef, Pork, and Lamb

Mongolian-Style Beef

Prep time: 10 minutes | Cook time: 10 minutes | Serves 4

INGREDIENTS

Oil, for spraying
450 g flank steak, thinly sliced
125 g soy sauce
1 tablespoon minced garlic
125 ml water
30 g cornflour
95 g Packed light brown sugar
2 teaspoons toasted sesame oil
½ teaspoon ground ginger
Cooked white rice or ramen noodles, for serving

DIRECTIONS

1. Line the air fryer basket with baking paper and spray lightly with oil.
2. Place the cornflour in a bowl and dredge the steak until evenly coated. Shake off any excess cornflour.
3. Place the steak in the prepared basket and spray lightly with oil.
4. Roast at 200°C for 5 minutes, flip, and cook for another 5 minutes.
5. In a small saucepan, combine the brown sugar, soy sauce, sesame oil, garlic, ginger, and water and bring to a boil over medium-high heat, stirring frequently. Remove from the heat.
6. Transfer the meat to the sauce and toss until evenly coated. Let sit for about 5 minutes so the steak absorbs the flavors. Serve with white rice or ramen noodles.

Beef and Tomato Sauce Meatloaf

Prep time: 15 minutes | Cook time: 25 minutes | Serves 4

INGREDIENTS

680 g minced beef
60 g breadcrumbs
60 g grated Parmesan cheese
2 tablespoons chopped parsley
2 garlic cloves, minced
1 teaspoon cayenne pepper
Cooking spray
250 g tomato sauce
2 egg whites
1 diced onion
2 tablespoons minced ginger
½ teaspoon dried basil
Salt and ground black pepper, to taste

DIRECTIONS

1. Preheat the air fryer to 180°C. Spritz a meatloaf pan with cooking spray.
2. Combine all the ingredients in a large bowl. Stir to mix well.
3. Pour the meat mixture in the prepared meatloaf pan and press with a spatula to make it firm.
4. Arrange the pan in the preheated air fryer and bake for 25 minutes or until the beef is well browned.
5. Serve immediately.

Sichuan Cumin Lamb

Prep time: 30 minutes | Cook time: 10 minutes | Serves 4

INGREDIENTS

Lamb:

2 tablespoons cumin seeds	1 teaspoon Sichuan peppercorns, or ½ teaspoon cayenne pepper
450 g lamb (preferably shoulder), cut into ½ by 2-inch pieces
2 tablespoons vegetable oil	1 tablespoon light soy sauce	1 tablespoon minced garlic
2 fresh red chillies, chopped	1 teaspoon kosher or coarse sea salt	¼ teaspoon sugar

For Serving:

2 spring onions, chopped	Large handful of chopped fresh coriander

DIRECTIONS

1. For the lamb: In a dry skillet, toast the cumin seeds and Sichuan peppercorns (if using) over medium heat, stirring frequently, until fragrant, 1 to 2 minutes. Remove from the heat and let cool. Use a mortar and pestle to coarsely grind the toasted spices.
2. Use a fork to pierce the lamb pieces to allow the marinade to penetrate better. In a large bowl or sandwich bag, combine the toasted spices, vegetable oil, soy sauce, garlic, chillies, salt, and sugar. Add the lamb to the bag. Seal and massage to coat. Marinate at room temperature for 30 minutes.
3. Place the lamb in a single layer in the air fryer basket. Set the air fryer to 176°C for 10 minutes. Use a meat thermometer to ensure the lamb has reached an internal temperature of 64°C (medium-rare).
4. Transfer the lamb to a serving bowl. Stir in the spring onions and coriander and serve.

Sausage and Peppers

Prep time: 7 minutes | Cook time: 35 minutes | Serves 4

INGREDIENTS

Oil, for spraying	910 g spicy or sweet Italian sausage links, cut into thick slices
4 large bell peppers of any color, seeded and cut into slices	1 onion, thinly sliced
1 tablespoon olive oil	1 tablespoon chopped fresh parsley	1 teaspoon dried oregano
1 teaspoon dried basil	1 teaspoon balsamic vinegar

DIRECTIONS

1. Line the air fryer basket with baking paper and spray lightly with oil.
2. In a large bowl, combine the sausage, bell peppers, and onion.
3. In a small bowl, whisk together the olive oil, parsley, oregano, basil, and balsamic vinegar. Pour the mixture over the sausage and peppers and toss until evenly coated.
4. Using a slotted spoon, transfer the mixture to the prepared basket, taking care to drain out as much excess liquid as possible.
5. Air fry at 176°C for 20 minutes, stir, and cook for another 15 minutes, or until the sausage is browned and the juices run clear.

Bacon-Wrapped Pork Tenderloin

Prep time: 30 minutes | Cook time: 22 to 25 minutes | Serves 6

INGREDIENTS

60 g minced onion
1 tablespoon minced garlic
¼ teaspoon freshly ground black pepper
1 to 2 tablespoons oil
125 ml hard apple cider, or apple juice
¼ teaspoon salt
910 g pork tenderloin
8 uncooked bacon slices
60 g honey

DIRECTIONS

1. In a medium bowl, stir together the onion, hard cider, honey, garlic, salt, and pepper. Transfer to a large sandwich bag or airtight container and add the pork. Seal the bag. Refrigerate to marinate for at least 2 hours.
2. Preheat the air fryer to 204°C. Line the air fryer basket with baking paper.
3. Remove the pork from the marinade and place it on the baking paper. Spritz with oil.
4. Cook for 15 minutes.
5. Wrap the bacon slices around the pork and secure them with toothpicks. Turn the pork roast and spritz with oil. Cook for 7 to 10 minutes more until the internal temperature reaches 64°C, depending on how well-done you like pork loin. It will continue cooking after it's removed from the fryer, so let it sit for 5 minutes before serving.

Herb-Crusted Lamb Chops

Prep time: 10 minutes | Cook time: 5 minutes | Serves 2

INGREDIENTS

1 large egg
30 g pork scratchings, ground to dust
1 tablespoon chopped fresh oregano leaves
1 teaspoon chopped fresh thyme leaves
4 (1-inch-thick) lamb chops
2 cloves garlic, minced
30 g powdered Parmesan cheese
1 tablespoon chopped fresh rosemary leaves
½ teaspoon ground black pepper

For Garnish/Serving (Optional):

Sprigs of fresh oregano
Sprigs of fresh thyme
Lemon slices
Sprigs of fresh rosemary
Lavender flowers

DIRECTIONS

1. Spray the air fryer basket with avocado oil. Preheat the air fryer to 204°C.
2. Beat the egg in a shallow bowl, add the garlic, and stir well to combine. In another shallow bowl, mix together the pork dust, Parmesan, herbs, and pepper.
3. One at a time, dip the lamb chops into the egg mixture, shake off the excess egg, and then dredge them in the Parmesan mixture. Use your hands to coat the chops well in the Parmesan mixture and form a nice crust on all sides; if necessary, dip the chops again in both the egg and the Parmesan mixture.
4. Place the lamb chops in the air fryer basket, leaving space between them, and air fry for 5

minutes, or until the internal temperature reaches 64°C for medium doneness. Allow to rest for 10 minutes before serving.

5. Garnish with sprigs of oregano, rosemary, and thyme, and lavender flowers, if desired. Serve with lemon slices, if desired.

6. Best served fresh. Store leftovers in an airtight container in the fridge for up to 4 days. Serve chilled over a salad, or reheat in a 176°C air fryer for 3 minutes, or until heated through.

Spaghetti Zoodles and Meatballs

Prep time: 30 minutes | Cook time: 11 to 13 minutes | Serves 6

INGREDIENTS

450 g minced beef

1 large egg, beaten

95 g Parmesan cheese

1 teaspoon Italian seasoning

Avocado oil spray

170 g courgette noodles, made using a spiraliser or store-bought

1½ teaspoons sea salt, plus more for seasoning

1 teaspoon gelatin

2 teaspoons minced garlic

Freshly ground black pepper, to taste

Keto-friendly marinara sauce, for serving

DIRECTIONS

1. Place the minced beef in a large bowl, and season with the salt.
2. Place the egg in a separate bowl and sprinkle with the gelatin. Allow to sit for 5 minutes.
3. Stir the gelatin mixture, then pour it over the minced beef. Add the Parmesan, garlic, and Italian seasoning. Season with salt and pepper.
4. Form the mixture into 1½-inch meatballs and place them on a plate; cover with plastic wrap and refrigerate for at least 1 hour or overnight.
5. Spray the meatballs with oil. Set the air fryer to 204°C and arrange the meatballs in a single layer in the air fryer basket. Air fry for 4 minutes. Flip the meatballs and spray them with more oil. Air fry for 4 minutes more, until an instant-read thermometer reads 72°C. Transfer the meatballs to a plate and allow them to rest.
6. While the meatballs are resting, heat the marinara in a saucepan on the stove over medium heat.
7. Place the courgette noodles in the air fryer, and cook at 204°C for 3 to 5 minutes.
8. To serve, place the courgette noodles in serving bowls. Top with meatballs and warm marinara.

Garlic Balsamic Beef

Prep time: 30 minutes | Cook time: 8 to 10 minutes | Serves 8

INGREDIENTS

910 g topside beef

3 tablespoons balsamic vinegar

2 tablespoons olive oil

½ teaspoon dried hot red pepper flakes

3 large garlic cloves, minced

3 tablespoons whole grain mustard

Sea salt and ground black pepper, to taste

DIRECTIONS

1. Score both sides of the cleaned beef.

2. Thoroughly combine the remaining ingredients; massage this mixture into the meat to coat it on all sides. Let it marinate for at least 3 hours.
3. Set the air fryer to 204°C; then cook the beef for 15 minutes. Flip it over and cook another 10 to 12 minutes. Bon appétit!

Beef Burger

Prep time: 20 minutes | Cook time: 12 minutes | Serves 4

INGREDIENTS

570 g lean minced beef
1 teaspoon Dijon mustard
1 teaspoon shallot powder
½ teaspoon cumin powder
⅓ teaspoon sea salt flakes
1 teaspoon celery seeds
1 tablespoon coconut aminos or tamari
A few dashes of liquid smoke
1 clove garlic, minced
30 g spring onions, minced
⅓ teaspoon freshly cracked mixed peppercorns
1 teaspoon parsley flakes

DIRECTIONS

1. Mix all of the above ingredients in a bowl; knead until everything is well incorporated.
2. Shape the mixture into four patties. Next, make a shallow dip in the center of each patty to prevent them puffing up during air frying.
3. Spritz the patties on all sides using nonstick cooking spray. Cook approximately 12 minutes at 184°C.
4. Check for doneness, an instant-read thermometer should read 72°C. Bon appétit!

Bacon, Cheese and Pear Stuffed Pork

Prep time: 10 minutes | Cook time: 24 minutes | Serves 3

INGREDIENTS

4 slices bacon, chopped
80 ml chicken stock
½ teaspoon dried thyme
1 pear, finely diced
3 boneless center-cut pork chops (2-inch thick)
Salt and freshly ground black pepper, to taste
1 tablespoon butter
185 g seasoned stuffing cubes
½ teaspoon salt
60 g finely diced onion
1 egg, beaten
⅛ teaspoon black pepper
40 g crumbled blue cheese
Olive oil

DIRECTIONS

1. Preheat the air fryer to 204°C.
2. Place the bacon into the air fryer basket and air fry for 6 minutes, stirring halfway through the cooking time. Remove the bacon and set it aside on a paper towel. Pour out the grease from the bottom of the air fryer.
3. Make the stuffing: Melt the butter in a medium saucepan over medium heat on the stovetop. Add the onion and sauté for a few minutes, until it starts to soften. Add the chicken stock and simmer for 1 minute. Remove the pan from the heat and add the stuffing cubes. Stir until the stock has been absorbed. Add the egg, dried thyme, salt and freshly ground black pepper, and stir until combined. Fold in the diced pear and crumbled blue cheese.

4. Place the pork chops on a cutting board. Using the palm of your hand to hold the chop flat and steady, slice into the side of the pork chop to make a pocket in the center of the chop. Leave about an inch of chop uncut and make sure you don't cut all the way through the pork chop. Brush both sides of the pork chops with olive oil and season with salt and freshly ground black pepper. Stuff each pork chop with a third of the stuffing, packing the stuffing tightly inside the pocket.
5. Preheat the air fryer to 184ºC.
6. Spray or brush the sides of the air fryer basket with oil. Place the pork chops in the air fryer basket with the open stuffed edge of the pork chop facing the outside edges of the basket.
7. Air fry the pork chops for 18 minutes, turning the pork chops over halfway through the cooking time. When the chops are done, let them rest for 5 minutes and then transfer to a serving platter.

Pork Medallions with Radicchio and Endive Salad

Prep time: 25 minutes | Cook time: 7 minutes | Serves 4

INGREDIENTS

1 (230 g) pork tenderloin
30 g plain flour
1 teaspoon paprika
1 teaspoon dried thyme

2 eggs, lightly beaten
1 teaspoon dry mustard
1 teaspoon salt

Salt and freshly ground black pepper, to taste
95 g matzo meal
1 teaspoon garlic powder
Vegetable or canola oil, in spray bottle

Vinaigrette:

65 ml white balsamic vinegar
1 tablespoon Dijon mustard
2 tablespoons chopped chervil or flat-leaf parsley
125 ml extra-virgin olive oil

2 tablespoons agave syrup (or honey or maple syrup)
Juice of ½ lemon
Salt and freshly ground black pepper

Radicchio and Endive Salad:

1 heart romaine lettuce, torn into large pieces
2 heads endive, sliced
85 g fresh Mozzarella, diced

½ head radicchio, coarsely chopped
60 g cherry tomatoes, halved
Salt and freshly ground black pepper, to taste

DIRECTIONS

1. Slice the pork tenderloin into 1-inch slices. Using a meat pounder, pound the pork slices into thin ½-inch medallions. Generously season the pork with salt and freshly ground black pepper on both sides.
2. Set up a dredging station using three shallow dishes. Put the flour in one dish and the beaten eggs in a second dish. Combine the matzo meal, paprika, dry mustard, garlic powder, thyme and salt in a third dish.
3. Preheat the air fryer to 204ºC.
4. Dredge the pork medallions in flour first and then into the beaten egg. Let the excess egg drip off and coat both sides of the medallions with the matzo meal crumb mixture. Spray both sides of the coated medallions with vegetable or canola oil.
5. Air fry the medallions in two batches at 204ºC for 5 minutes. Once you have air-fried all the medallions, flip them all over and return the first batch of medallions back into the air fryer on top of the second batch. Air fry at 204ºC for an additional 2 minutes.
6. While the medallions are cooking, make the salad and dressing. Whisk the white balsamic vinegar, agave syrup, Dijon mustard, lemon juice, chervil, salt and pepper together in a small bowl.

Whisk in the olive oil slowly until combined and thickened.

7. Combine the romaine lettuce, radicchio, endive, cherry tomatoes, and Mozzarella cheese in a large salad bowl. Drizzle the dressing over the vegetables and toss to combine. Season with salt and freshly ground black pepper.

8. Serve the pork medallions warm on or beside the salad.

Smothered Chops

Prep time: 20 minutes | Cook time: 30 minutes | Serves 4

INGREDIENTS

4 bone-in pork chops (230 g each)
1½ teaspoons freshly ground black pepper, divided
250 g tomato purée
1 tablespoon sugar
60 g chopped onion
1 to 2 tablespoons oil
2 teaspoons salt, divided
1 teaspoon garlic powder
1½ teaspoons Italian seasoning
1 tablespoon cornflour
60 g chopped green bell pepper

DIRECTIONS

1. Evenly season the pork chops with 1 teaspoon salt, 1 teaspoon pepper, and the garlic powder.

2. In a medium bowl, stir together the tomato purée, Italian seasoning, sugar, remaining 1 teaspoon of salt, and remaining ½ teaspoon of pepper.

3. In a small bowl, whisk 185 ml water and the cornflour until blended. Stir this slurry into the tomato purée, with the onion and green bell pepper. Transfer to a baking pan.

4. Preheat the air fryer to 176°C.

5. Place the sauce in the fryer and cook for 10 minutes. Stir and cook for 10 minutes more. Remove the pan and keep warm.

6. Increase the air fryer temperature to 204°C. Line the air fryer basket with baking paper.

7. Place the pork chops on the baking paper and spritz with oil.

8. Cook for 5 minutes. Flip and spritz the chops with oil and cook for 5 minutes more, until the internal temperature reaches 64°C. Serve with the tomato mixture spooned on top.

Air Fryer Chicken-Fried Steak

Prep time: 5 minutes | Cook time: 20 minutes | Serves 4

INGREDIENTS

455 g beef sirloin steak
1 teaspoon dried rosemary
60 g coconut flour
750 ml skimmed milk, divided
2 medium egg whites
1 tablespoon Creole seasoning
1 teaspoon dried thyme
125 g chickpea crumbs

DIRECTIONS

1. In a bowl, marinate the steak in 500 ml milk for 30 to 45 minutes.

2. Remove the steak from milk, shake off the excess liquid, and season with the thyme and rosemary. Discard the milk.

3. In a shallow bowl, beat the egg whites with the remaining 250 ml milk.

4. In a separate shallow bowl, combine the chickpea crumbs, coconut flour, and seasoning.
5. Dip the steak in the egg white mixture then dredge in the chickpea crumb mixture, coating well.
6. Place the steak in the basket of an air fryer.
7. Set the air fryer to 390°F, close, and cook for 10 minutes.
8. Open the air fryer, turn the steaks, close, and cook for 10 minutes. Let rest for 5 minutes.

Herb-Roasted Beef Tips with Onions

Prep time: 5 minutes | Cook time: 10 minutes | Serves 4

INGREDIENTS

455 g rib eye steak, cubed
1 tablespoon fresh oregano
1 yellow onion, thinly sliced
2 garlic cloves, minced
1 teaspoon salt
2 tablespoons olive oil
½ teaspoon black pepper

DIRECTIONS

1. Preheat the air fryer to 192°C.
2. In a medium bowl, combine the steak, garlic, olive oil, oregano, salt, pepper, and onion. Mix until all of the beef and onion are well coated.
3. Put the seasoned steak mixture into the air fryer basket. Roast for 5 minutes. Stir and roast for 5 minutes more.
4. Let rest for 5 minutes before serving with some favorite sides.

Blackened Cajun Pork Roast

Prep time: 20 minutes | Cook time: 33 minutes | Serves 4

INGREDIENTS

910 g bone-in pork loin roast
60 g diced onion
1 tablespoon minced garlic
2 tablespoons oil
10 g diced celery
30 g Cajun seasoning
60 g diced green bell pepper

DIRECTIONS

1. Cut 5 slits across the pork roast. Spritz it with oil, coating it completely. Evenly sprinkle the Cajun seasoning over the pork roast.
2. In a medium bowl, stir together the onion, celery, green bell pepper, and garlic until combined. Set aside.
3. Preheat the air fryer to 184°C. Line the air fryer basket with baking paper.
4. Place the pork roast on the baking paper and spritz with oil.
5. Cook for 5 minutes. Flip the roast and cook for 5 minutes more. Continue to flip and cook in 5-minute increments for a total cook time of 20 minutes.
6. Increase the air fryer temperature to 200°C.
7. Cook the roast for 8 minutes more and flip. Add the vegetable mixture to the basket and cook for a final 5 minutes. Let the roast sit for 5 minutes before serving.

Bacon-Wrapped Cheese Pork

Prep time: 10 minutes | Cook time: 20 minutes | Serves 4

INGREDIENTS

4 (1-inch-thick) boneless pork chops
8 slices thin-cut bacon
2 (150 g) packages Boursin cheese
Avocado oil for spraying

DIRECTIONS

1. Spray the air fryer basket with avocado oil. Preheat the air fryer to 204°C.
2. Place one of the chops on a cutting board. With a sharp knife held parallel to the cutting board, make a 1-inch-wide incision on the top edge of the chop. Carefully cut into the chop to form a large pocket, leaving a ½-inch border along the sides and bottom. Repeat with the other 3 chops.
3. Snip the corner of a large resealable sandwich bag to form a ¾-inch hole. Place the Boursin cheese in the bag and pipe the cheese into the pockets in the chops, dividing the cheese evenly among them.
4. Wrap 2 slices of bacon around each chop and secure the ends with toothpicks. Place the bacon-wrapped chops in the air fryer basket and cook for 10 minutes, then flip the chops and cook for another 8 to 10 minutes, until the bacon is crisp, the chops are cooked through, and the internal temperature reaches 64°C.
5. Store leftovers in an airtight container in the refrigerator for up to 3 days. Reheat in a preheated 204°C air fryer for 5 minutes, or until warmed through.

Pork Tenderloin with Avocado Lime Sauce

Prep time: 30 minutes | Cook time: 15 minutes | Serves 4

INGREDIENTS

Marinade:

125 ml lime juice
2 teaspoons granulated sweetener, or ¼ teaspoon liquid sweetener
1½ teaspoons fine sea salt
1 teaspoon smoked paprika
Grated zest of 1 lime
3 cloves garlic, minced
1 teaspoon chilli powder, or more for more heat
455 g pork tenderloin

Avocado Lime Sauce:

1 medium-sized ripe avocado, roughly chopped
125 g full-fat sour cream (or coconut cream for dairy-free)
Grated zest of 1 lime
2 cloves garlic, roughly chopped
¼ teaspoon ground black pepper
Lime slices, for serving
Juice of 1 lime
½ teaspoon fine sea salt
Chopped fresh coriander leaves, for garnish
Pico de Gallo, for serving

DIRECTIONS

1. In a medium-sized casserole dish, stir together all the marinade ingredients until well combined. Add the tenderloin and coat it well in the marinade. Cover and place in the fridge to marinate for 2 hours or overnight.
2. Spray the air fryer basket with avocado oil. Preheat the air fryer to 204°C.
3. Remove the pork from the marinade and place it in the air fryer basket. Air fry for 13 to 15

minutes, until the internal temperature of the pork is 64°C, flipping after 7 minutes. Remove the pork from the air fryer and place it on a cutting board. Allow it to rest for 8 to 10 minutes, then cut it into ½-inch-thick slices.

4. While the pork cooks, make the avocado lime sauce: Place all the sauce ingredients in a food processor and purée until smooth. Taste and adjust the seasoning to your liking.

5. Place the pork slices on a serving platter and spoon the avocado lime sauce on top. Garnish with coriander leaves and serve with lime slices and Pico de Gallo.

6. Store leftovers in an airtight container in the fridge for up to 4 days. Reheat in a preheated 204°C air fryer for 5 minutes, or until heated through.

Chapter 6 Snacks and Appetisers

Aubergine Fries

Prep time: 10 minutes | Cook time: 7 to 8 minutes per batch | Serves 4

INGREDIENTS

1 medium aubergine
1 teaspoon garlic powder
1 large egg
1 teaspoon ground coriander
½ teaspoon salt
2 tablespoons water
1 teaspoon cumin
125 g crushed panko bread crumbs
Oil for misting or cooking spray

DIRECTIONS

1. Peel and cut the aubergine into fat fries, ⅜- to ½-inch thick.
2. Preheat the air fryer to 200°C.
3. In a small cup, mix together the coriander, cumin, garlic, and salt.
4. Combine 1 teaspoon of the seasoning mix and panko crumbs in a shallow dish.
5. Place aubergine fries in a large bowl, sprinkle with remaining seasoning, and stir well to combine.
6. Beat eggs and water together and pour over aubergine fries. Stir to coat.
7. Remove aubergine from egg wash, shaking off excess, and roll in panko crumbs.
8. Spray with oil.
9. Place half of the fries in air fryer basket. You should have only a single layer, but it's fine if they overlap a little.
10. Cook for 5 minutes. Shake basket, mist lightly with oil, and cook 2 to 3 minutes longer, until browned and crispy.
11. Repeat step 10 to cook remaining eggplant.

Crispy Breaded Beef Cubes

Prep time: 10 minutes | Cook time: 12 to 16 minutes | Serves 4

INGREDIENTS

450 g sirloin tip, cut into 1-inch cubes
2 tablespoons olive oil
250 g cheese pasta sauce
½ teaspoon dried marjoram
185 g soft bread crumbs

DIRECTIONS

1. Preheat the air fryer to 180°C.
2. In a medium bowl, toss the beef with the pasta sauce to coat.
3. In a shallow bowl, combine the bread crumbs, oil, and marjoram, and mix well. Drop the beef cubes, one at a time, into the bread crumb mixture to coat thoroughly.
4. Air fry the beef in two batches for 6 to 8 minutes, shaking the basket once during cooking time, until the beef is at least 64°C and the outside is crisp and brown.
5. Serve hot.

Shishito Peppers with Herb Dressing

Prep time: 10 minutes | Cook time: 6 minutes | Serves 2 to 4

INGREDIENTS

170 g Shishito peppers

Kosher or coarse sea salt and freshly ground black pepper, to taste

2 tablespoons finely chopped fresh basil leaves

1 tablespoon finely chopped fresh tarragon

Finely grated zest of ½ lemon

Flaky sea salt, for serving

1 tablespoon vegetable oil

125 g mayonnaise

2 tablespoons finely chopped fresh flat-leaf parsley

1 tablespoon finely chopped fresh chives

1 tablespoon fresh lemon juice

DIRECTIONS

1. Preheat the air fryer to 204°C.
2. In a bowl, toss together the Shishitos and oil to evenly coat and season with kosher salt and black pepper. Transfer to the air fryer and air fry for 6 minutes, shaking the basket halfway through, or until the Shishitos are blistered and lightly charred.
3. Meanwhile, in a small bowl, whisk together the mayonnaise, basil, parsley, tarragon, chives, lemon zest, and lemon juice.
4. Pile the peppers on a plate, sprinkle with flaky sea salt, and serve hot with the dressing.

Carrot Chips

Prep time: 15 minutes | Cook time: 8 to 10 minutes | Serves 4

INGREDIENTS

1 tablespoon olive oil, plus more for greasing the basket

4 to 5 medium carrots, trimmed and thinly sliced

1 teaspoon seasoned salt

DIRECTIONS

1. Preheat the air fryer to 200°C. Grease the air fryer basket with the olive oil.
2. Toss the carrot slices with 1 tablespoon of olive oil and salt in a medium bowl until thoroughly coated.
3. Arrange the carrot slices in the greased basket. You may need to work in batches to avoid overcrowding.
4. Air fry for 8 to 10 minutes until the carrot slices are crisp-tender. Shake the basket once during cooking.
5. Transfer the carrot slices to a bowl and repeat with the remaining carrots.
6. Allow to cool for 5 minutes and serve.

Crunchy Tex-Mex Tortilla Chips

Prep time: 5 minutes | Cook time: 5 minutes | Serves 4

INGREDIENTS

Olive oil

½ teaspoon chilli powder

8 (6-inch) corn tortillas, each cut into 6 wedges

½ teaspoon salt

½ teaspoon paprika

½ teaspoon ground cumin

Pinch cayenne pepper

DIRECTIONS

1. Spray fryer basket lightly with olive oil.
2. In a small bowl, combine the salt, cumin, chilli powder, paprika, and cayenne pepper.
3. Place the tortilla wedges in the air fryer basket in a single layer. Spray the tortillas lightly with oil and sprinkle with some of the seasoning mixture. You will need to cook the tortillas in batches.
4. Air fry at 192°C for 2 to 3 minutes. Shake the basket and cook until the chips are light brown and crispy, an additional 2 to 3 minutes. Watch the chips closely so they do not burn.

Lemony Endive in Curried Yogurt

Prep time: 5 minutes | Cook time: 10 minutes | Serves 6

INGREDIENTS

6 heads endive
1 teaspoon garlic powder
125 ml plain and fat-free yogurt
½ teaspoon curry powder
3 tablespoons lemon juice
Salt and ground black pepper, to taste

DIRECTIONS

1. Wash the endives, and slice them in half lengthwise.
2. In a bowl, mix together the yogurt, lemon juice, garlic powder, curry powder, salt and pepper.
3. Brush the endive halves with the marinade, coating them completely. Allow to sit for at least 30 minutes or up to 24 hours.
4. Preheat the air fryer to 160°C.
5. Put the endives in the air fryer basket and air fry for 10 minutes.
6. Serve hot.

Lemon-Pepper Chicken Drumsticks

Prep time: 30 minutes | Cook time: 30 minutes | Serves 2

INGREDIENTS

2 teaspoons freshly ground coarse black pepper
½ teaspoon garlic powder
Kosher or coarse sea salt, to taste
1 teaspoon baking powder
4 chicken drumsticks (115 g each)
1 lemon

DIRECTIONS

1. In a small bowl, stir together the pepper, baking powder, and garlic powder. Place the drumsticks on a plate and sprinkle evenly with the baking powder mixture, turning the drumsticks so they're well coated. Let the drumsticks stand in the refrigerator for at least 1 hour or up to overnight.
2. Sprinkle the drumsticks with salt, then transfer them to the air fryer, standing them bone-end up and leaning against the wall of the air fryer basket. Air fry at 192°C until cooked through and crisp on the outside, about 30 minutes.
3. Transfer the drumsticks to a serving platter and finely grate the zest of the lemon over them while they're hot. Cut the lemon into wedges and serve with the warm drumsticks.

Cheesy Steak Fries

Prep time: 5 minutes | Cook time: 20 minutes | Serves 5

INGREDIENTS
1 (800 g) bag frozen steak-cut fries
Cooking spray
Salt and pepper, to taste
125 g beef gravy
125 g shredded Mozzarella cheese
2 spring onions, green parts only, chopped

DIRECTIONS
1. Preheat the air fryer to 204°C.
2. Place the frozen steak-cut fries in the air fryer. Air fry for 10 minutes. Shake the basket and spritz the fries with cooking spray. Sprinkle with salt and pepper. Air fry for an additional 8 minutes.
3. Pour the beef gravy into a medium, microwave-safe bowl. Microwave for 30 seconds, or until the gravy is warm.
4. Sprinkle the fries with the cheese. Air fry for an additional 2 minutes, until the cheese is melted.
5. Transfer the fries to a serving dish. Drizzle the fries with gravy and sprinkle the spring onions on top for a green garnish. Serve.

Black Bean Corn Dip

Prep time: 10 minutes | Cook time: 10 minutes | Serves 4

INGREDIENTS
½ (425 g) can black beans, drained and rinsed
½ (425 g) can sweetcorn, drained and rinsed
60 g chunky salsa
60 g reduced-fat cream cheese, softened
30 g shredded reduced-fat Cheddar cheese
½ teaspoon ground cumin
½ teaspoon paprika
Salt and freshly ground black pepper, to taste

DIRECTIONS
1. Preheat the air fryer to 164°C.
2. In a medium bowl, mix together the black beans, sweetcorn, salsa, cream cheese, Cheddar cheese, cumin, and paprikSeason with salt and pepper and stir until well combined.
3. Spoon the mixture into a baking dish.
4. Place baking dish in the air fryer basket and bake until heated through, about 10 minutes.
5. Serve hot.

Golden Onion Rings

Prep time: 15 minutes | Cook time: 14 minutes per batch | Serves 4

INGREDIENTS

1 large white onion, peeled and cut into ½ to ¾-inch-thick slices
125 ml skimmed milk
125 g whole-wheat pastry flour, or plain flour
2 tablespoons cornflour
¾ teaspoon sea salt, divided
½ teaspoon freshly ground black pepper, divided
¾ teaspoon granulated garlic, divided
185 g whole grain bread crumbs, or gluten-free bread crumbs
Cooking oil spray (coconut, sunflower, or safflower)
Ketchup, for serving (optional)

DIRECTIONS

1. Carefully separate the onion slices into rings—a gentle touch is important here.
2. Place the milk in a shallow bowl and set aside.
3. Make the first breading: In a medium bowl, stir together the flour, cornflour, ¼ teaspoon of salt, ¼ teaspoon of pepper, and ¼ teaspoon of granulated garlic. Set aside.
4. Make the second breading: In a separate medium bowl, stir together the bread crumbs with the remaining ½ teaspoon of salt, the remaining ½ teaspoon of garlic, and the remaining ½ teaspoon of pepper. Set aside.
5. Insert the crisper plate into the basket and the basket into the unit. Preheat the unit by selecting AIR FRY, setting the temperature to 200°C, and setting the time to 3 minutes. Select START/STOP to begin.
6. Once the unit is preheated, spray the crisper plate and the basket with cooking oil.
7. To make the onion rings, dip one ring into the milk and into the first breading mixture. Dip the ring into the milk again and back into the first breading mixture, coating thoroughly. Dip the ring into the milk one last time and then into the second breading mixture, coating thoroughly. Gently lay the onion ring in the basket. Repeat with additional rings and, as you place them into the basket, do not overlap them too much. Once all the onion rings are in the basket, generously spray the tops with cooking oil.
8. Select AIR FRY, set the temperature to 200°C, and set the time to 14 minutes. Insert the basket into the unit. Select START/STOP to begin.
9. After 4 minutes, open the unit and spray the rings generously with cooking oil. Close the unit to resume cooking. After 3 minutes, remove the basket and spray the onion rings again. Remove the rings, turn them over, and place them back into the basket. Generously spray them again with oil. Reinsert the basket to resume cooking. After 4 minutes, generously spray the rings with oil one last time. Resume cooking for the remaining 3 minutes, or until the onion rings are very crunchy and brown.
10. When the cooking is complete, serve the hot rings with ketchup, or other sauce of choice.

Bruschetta with Basil Pesto

Prep time: 10 minutes | Cook time: 5 to 11 minutes | Serves 4

INGREDIENTS

8 slices French bread, ½ inch thick
125 g shredded Mozzarella cheese
125 g chopped grape tomatoes

2 tablespoons softened butter
125 g basil pesto
2 spring onions, thinly sliced

DIRECTIONS

1. Preheat the air fryer to 176°C.
2. Spread the bread with the butter and place butter-side up in the air fryer basket. Bake for 3 to 5 minutes, or until the bread is light golden brown.
3. Remove the bread from the basket and top each piece with some of the cheese. Return to the basket in 2 batches and bake for 1 to 3 minutes, or until the cheese melts.
4. Meanwhile, combine the pesto, tomatoes, and spring onions in a small bowl.
5. When the cheese has melted, remove the bread from the air fryer and place on a serving plate. Top each slice with some of the pesto mixture and serve.

Stuffed Figs with Goat Cheese and Honey

Prep time: 5 minutes | Cook time: 10 minutes | Serves 4

INGREDIENTS

8 fresh figs
1 tablespoon honey, plus more for serving
60 g goat cheese
1 tablespoon olive oil
¼ teaspoon ground cinnamon

DIRECTIONS

1. Preheat the air fryer to 184°C.
2. Cut the stem off of each fig.
3. Cut an X into the top of each fig, cutting halfway down the fig. Leave the base intact.
4. In a small bowl, mix together the goat cheese, cinnamon, and honey.
5. Spoon the goat cheese mixture into the cavity of each fig.
6. Place the figs in a single layer in the air fryer basket. Drizzle the olive oil over top of the figs and roast for 10 minutes.
7. Serve with an additional drizzle of honey.

Courgette Fries with Roasted Garlic Aïoli

Prep time: 20 minutes | Cook time: 12 minutes | Serves 4

INGREDIENTS

1 tablespoon vegetable oil
½ head green or savoy cabbage, finely shredded

Roasted Garlic Aïoli:

1 teaspoon roasted garlic
Juice of ½ lemon
125 g mayonnaise
Salt and pepper, to taste
2 tablespoons olive oil

Courgette Fries:

60 g plain flour
Salt and pepper, to taste
2 eggs, beaten
1 large courgette, cut into ½-inch sticks
125 g seasoned bread crumbs
Olive oil

DIRECTIONS

1. Make the aïoli: Combine the roasted garlic, mayonnaise, olive oil and lemon juice in a bowl and whisk well. Season the aïoli with salt and pepper to taste.
2. Prepare the courgette fries. Create a dredging station with three shallow dishes. Place the flour in the first shallow dish and season well with salt and freshly ground black pepper. Put the beaten eggs in the second shallow dish. In the third shallow dish, combine the bread crumbs, salt and pepper. Dredge the courgette sticks, coating with flour first, then dipping them into the eggs to coat, and finally tossing in bread crumbs. Shake the dish with the bread crumbs and pat the crumbs onto the courgette sticks gently with your hands so they stick evenly.
3. Place the courgette fries on a flat surface and let them sit at least 10 minutes before air frying to let them dry out a little. Preheat the air fryer to 204°C.
4. Spray the courgette sticks with olive oil, and place them into the air fryer basket. You can air fry the courgette in two layers, placing the second layer in the opposite direction to the first. Air fry for 12 minutes turning and rotating the fries halfway through the cooking time. Spray with additional oil when you turn them over.
5. Serve courgette fries warm with the roasted garlic aïoli.

Dark Chocolate and Cranberry Granola Bars

Prep time: 5 minutes | Cook time: 15 minutes | Serves 6

INGREDIENTS

250 g certified gluten-free quick oats
2 tablespoons unsweetened dried cranberries
125 g raw honey
⅛ teaspoon salt
2 tablespoons sugar-free dark chocolate chunks
3 tablespoons unsweetened desiccated coconut
1 teaspoon ground cinnamon
2 tablespoons olive oil

DIRECTIONS

1. Preheat the air fryer to 184°C. Line an 8-by-8-inch baking dish with baking paper that comes up the side so you can lift it out after cooking.
2. In a large bowl, mix together all of the ingredients until well combined.
3. Press the oat mixture into the pan in an even layer.
4. Place the pan into the air fryer basket and bake for 15 minutes.
5. Remove the pan from the air fryer, and lift the granola cake out of the pan using the edges of the baking paper.
6. Allow to cool for 5 minutes before slicing into 6 equal bars.
7. Serve immediately, or wrap in plastic wrap and store at room temperature for up to 1 week.

Caramelised Onion Dip

Prep time: 5 minutes | Cook time: 30 minutes | Serves 8 to 10

INGREDIENTS

1 tablespoon butter

1 medium yellow onion, halved and thinly sliced

¼ teaspoon kosher or coarse sea salt, plus additional for seasoning

110 g cream cheese, softened

125 g sour cream

¼ teaspoon onion powder

1 tablespoon chopped fresh chives

Black pepper, to taste

Thick-cut potato chips or vegetable chips

DIRECTIONS

1. Place the butter in a baking pan. Place the pan in the air fryer basket. Set the air fryer to 92°C for 1 minute, or until the butter is melted. Add the onions and salt to the pan.
2. Set the air fryer to 92°C for 15 minutes, or until onions are softened. Set the air fryer to 192°C for 15 minutes, until onions are a deep golden brown, stirring two or three times during the cooking time. Let cool completely.
3. In a medium bowl, stir together the cooked onions, cream cheese, sour cream, onion powder, and chives. Season with salt and pepper. Cover and refrigerate for 2 hours to allow the flavors to blend.
4. Serve the dip with potato chips or vegetable chips.

Ranch Oyster Snack Crackers

Prep time: 3 minutes | Cook time: 12 minutes | Serves 6

INGREDIENTS

Oil, for spraying

65 ml olive oil

2 teaspoons dry ranch seasoning

1 teaspoon chilli powder

½ teaspoon dried dill

½ teaspoon garlic granules

½ teaspoon salt

1 (255 g) bag oyster crackers

DIRECTIONS

1. Preheat the air fryer to 164°C. Line the air fryer basket with baking paper and spray lightly with oil.
2. In a large bowl, mix together the olive oil, ranch seasoning, chilli powder, dill, garlic, and salt. Add the crackers and toss until evenly coated.
3. Place the mixture in the prepared basket.
4. Cook for 10 to 12 minutes, shaking or stirring every 3 to 4 minutes, or until crisp and golden brown.

Lemony Pear Chips

Prep time: 15 minutes | Cook time: 9 to 13 minutes | Serves 4

INGREDIENTS

2 firm Bosc pears, cut crosswise into ⅛-inch-thick slices

1 tablespoon freshly squeezed lemon juice

½ teaspoon ground cinnamon

⅛ teaspoon ground cardamom

DIRECTIONS

1. Preheat the air fryer to 192°C.
2. Separate the smaller stem-end pear rounds from the larger rounds with seeds. Remove the core and seeds from the larger slices. Sprinkle all slices with lemon juice, cinnamon, and cardamom.
3. Put the smaller chips into the air fryer basket. Air fry for 3 to 5 minutes, or until light golden brown, shaking the basket once during cooking. Remove from the air fryer.
4. Repeat with the larger slices, air frying for 6 to 8 minutes, or until light golden brown, shaking the basket once during cooking.
5. Remove the chips from the air fryer. Cool and serve or store in an airtight container at room temperature up for to 2 days.

Crunchy Chickpeas

Prep time: 5 minutes | Cook time: 15 to 20 minutes | Serves 4

INGREDIENTS

½ teaspoon chilli powder
½ teaspoon ground cumin
¼ teaspoon cayenne pepper
¼ teaspoon salt
1 (540 g) can chickpeas, drained and rinsed
Cooking spray

DIRECTIONS

1. Preheat the air fryer to 200°C. Lightly spritz the air fryer basket with cooking spray.
2. Mix the chilli powder, cumin, cayenne pepper, and salt in a small bowl.
3. Place the chickpeas in a medium bowl and lightly mist with cooking spray.
4. Add the spice mixture to the chickpeas and toss until evenly coated.
5. Place the chickpeas in the air fryer basket and air fry for 15 to 20 minutes, or until the chickpeas are cooked to your preferred crunchiness. Shake the basket three or four times during cooking.
6. Let the chickpeas cool for 5 minutes before serving.

Classic Spring Rolls

Prep time: 10 minutes | Cook time: 9 minutes | Makes 16 spring rolls

INGREDIENTS

4 teaspoons toasted sesame oil
1 tablespoon grated peeled fresh ginger
500 g chopped green or Savoy cabbage
½ teaspoon sea salt
6 medium garlic cloves, minced or pressed
250 g thinly sliced shiitake mushrooms
125 g grated carrot
16 rice paper wrappers
Cooking oil spray (sunflower, safflower, or refined coconut)
Gluten-free sweet and sour sauce or Thai sweet chilli sauce, for serving (optional)

DIRECTIONS

1. Place a wok or sauté pan over medium heat until hot.
2. Add the sesame oil, garlic, ginger, mushrooms, cabbage, carrot, and salt. Cook for 3 to 4 minutes, stirring often, until the cabbage is lightly wilted. Remove the pan from the heat.
3. Gently run a rice paper under water. Lay it on a flat nonabsorbent surface. Place about 60 g cabbage filling in the middle. Once the wrapper is soft enough to roll, fold the bottom up over the

filling, fold in the sides, and roll the wrapper all the way up. (Basically, make a tiny burrito.) 4. Repeat step 3 to make the remaining spring rolls until you have the number of spring rolls you want to cook right now (and the amount that will fit in the air fryer basket in a single layer without them touching each other). Refrigerate any leftover filling in an airtight container for about 1 week.

5. Insert the crisper plate into the basket and the basket into the unit. Preheat the unit by selecting AIR FRY, setting the temperature to 200°C, and setting the time to 3 minutes. Select START/STOP to begin.

6. Once the unit is preheated, spray the crisper plate and the basket with cooking oil. Place the spring rolls into the basket, leaving a little room between them so they don't stick to each other. Spray the top of each spring roll with cooking oil.

7. Select AIR FRY, set the temperature to 200°C, and set the time to 9 minutes. Select START/STOP to begin.

8. When the cooking is complete, the egg rolls should be crisp-ish and lightly browned. Serve immediately, plain or with a sauce of choice.

Asian Five-Spice Wings

Prep time: 30 minutes | Cook time: 13 to 15 minutes | Serves 4

INGREDIENTS

910 g chicken wings

2 tablespoons Chinese five-spice powder

125 g Asian-style salad dressing

DIRECTIONS

1. Cut off wing tips and discard or freeze for stock. Cut remaining wing pieces in two at the joint.
2. Place wing pieces in a large sealable plastic bag. Pour in the Asian dressing, seal bag, and massage the marinade into the wings until well coated. Refrigerate for at least an hour.
3. Remove wings from bag, drain off excess marinade, and place wings in air fryer basket.
4. Air fry at 184°C for 13 to 15 minutes or until juices run clear. About halfway through cooking time, shake the basket or stir wings for more even cooking.
5. Transfer cooked wings to plate in a single layer. Sprinkle half of the Chinese five-spice powder on the wings, turn, and sprinkle other side with remaining seasoning.

Old Bay Chicken Wings

Prep time: 10 minutes | Cook time: 12 to 15 minutes | Serves 4

INGREDIENTS

2 tablespoons Old Bay seasoning

2 teaspoons salt

2 teaspoons baking powder

910 g chicken wings, patted dry

Cooking spray

DIRECTIONS

1. Preheat the air fryer to 204°C. Lightly spray the air fryer basket with cooking spray.
2. Combine the Old Bay seasoning, baking powder, and salt in a large sandwich bag. Add the chicken wings, seal, and shake until the wings are thoroughly coated in the seasoning mixture.
3. Lay the chicken wings in the air fryer basket in a single layer and lightly mist with cooking spray.

You may need to work in batches to avoid overcrowding.
4. Air fry for 12 to 15 minutes, flipping the wings halfway through, or until the wings are lightly browned and the internal temperature reaches at least 76°C on a meat thermometer.
5. Remove from the basket to a plate and repeat with the remaining chicken wings.
6. Serve hot.

Chapter 7 Desserts

Cinnamon and Pecan Pie

Prep time: 10 minutes | Cook time: 25 minutes | Serves 4

INGREDIENTS

1 pie case
2 eggs
3 tablespoons melted butter, divided
½ teaspoons cinnamon
185 g maple syrup
2 tablespoons sugar
¾ teaspoon vanilla extract
⅛ teaspoon nutmeg
60 g chopped pecans

DIRECTIONS

1. Preheat the air fryer to 188ºC.
2. In a small bowl, coat the pecans in 1 tablespoon of melted butter.
3. Transfer the pecans to the air fryer and air fry for about 10 minutes.
4. Put the pie dough in a greased pie pan and add the pecans on top.
5. In a bowl, mix the rest of the ingredients. Pour this over the pecans.
6. Put the pan in the air fryer and bake for 25 minutes.
7. Serve immediately.

Olive Oil Cake

Prep time: 10 minutes | Cook time: 30 minutes | Serves 8

INGREDIENTS

250 g blanched finely ground almond flour
185 ml extra-virgin olive oil
1 teaspoon vanilla extract
5 large eggs, whisked
40 g granulated sweetener
1 teaspoon baking powder

DIRECTIONS

1. In a large bowl, mix all ingredients. Pour batter into an ungreased round nonstick baking dish.
2. Place dish into air fryer basket. Adjust the temperature to 148ºC and bake for 30 minutes. The cake will be golden on top and firm in the center when done.
3. Let cake cool in dish 30 minutes before slicing and serving.

Rhubarb and Strawberry Crumble

Prep time: 10 minutes | Cook time: 12 to 17 minutes | Serves 6

INGREDIENTS

185 g sliced fresh strawberries
80 g quick-cooking oatmeal
30 g packed light brown sugar
3 tablespoons unsalted butter, melted
15 g sliced rhubarb
60 g whole-wheat pastry flour, or plain flour
½ teaspoon ground cinnamon
40 g granulated sugar

DIRECTIONS

1. Insert the crisper plate into the basket and the basket into the unit. Preheat the unit by selecting

BAKE, setting the temperature to 192ºC, and setting the time to 3 minutes. Select START/STOP to begin.

2. In a 6-by-2-inch round metal baking pan, combine the strawberries, rhubarb, and granulated sugar.

3. In a medium bowl, stir together the oatmeal, flour, brown sugar, and cinnamon. Stir the melted butter into this mixture until crumbly. Sprinkle the crumble mixture over the fruit.

4. Once the unit is preheated, place the pan into the basket.

5. Select BAKE, set the temperature to 192ºC, and set the time to 17 minutes. Select START/STOP to begin.

6. After about 12 minutes, check the crumble. If the fruit is bubbling and the topping is golden brown, it is done. If not, resume cooking.

7. When the cooking is complete, serve warm.

Blackberry Cobbler

Prep time: 15 minutes | Cook time: 25 to 30 minutes | Serves 6

INGREDIENTS

375 g fresh or frozen blackberries
8 tablespoons butter, melted
220 g sugar, divided
125 g self-raising flour
1 teaspoon vanilla extract
1 to 2 tablespoons oil

DIRECTIONS

1. In a medium bowl, stir together the blackberries, 125 g sugar, and vanill2. In another medium bowl, stir together the melted butter, remaining 95 g sugar, and flour until a dough forms.

3. Spritz a baking pan with oil. Add the blackberry mixture. Crumble the flour mixture over the fruit. Cover the pan with aluminum foil.

4. Preheat the air fryer to 176ºC.

5. Place the covered pan in the air fryer basket. Cook for 20 to 25 minutes until the filling is thickened.

6. Uncover the pan and cook for 5 minutes more, depending on how juicy and browned you like your cobbler. Let sit for 5 minutes before serving.

Apple Hand Pies

Prep time: 15 minutes | Cook time: 25 minutes | Serves 8

INGREDIENTS

2 apples, cored and diced
1 teaspoon vanilla extract
1 teaspoon water
60 g honey
⅛ teaspoon ground nutmeg
4 refrigerated piecrusts
1 teaspoon ground cinnamon
2 teaspoons cornflour
Cooking oil spray

DIRECTIONS

1. Insert the crisper plate into the basket and the basket into the unit. Preheat the unit by selecting AIR FRY, setting the temperature to 204ºC, and setting the time to 3 minutes. Select START/STOP to begin.

2. In a metal bowl that fits into the basket, stir together the apples, honey, cinnamon, vanilla, and nutmeg.

3. In a small bowl, whisk the cornflour and water until the cornflour dissolves.

4. Once the unit is preheated, place the metal bowl with the apples into the basket.

5. Select AIR FRY, set the temperature to 204°C, and set the time to 5 minutes. Select START/STOP to begin.

6. After 2 minutes, stir the apples. Resume cooking for 2 minutes.

7. Remove the bowl and stir the cornflour mixture into the apples. Reinsert the metal bowl into the basket and resume cooking for about 30 seconds until the sauce thickens slightly.

8. When the cooking is complete, refrigerate the apples while you prepare the piecrust.

9. Cut each piecrust into 2 (4-inch) circles. You should have 8 circles of crust.

10. Lay the piecrusts on a work surface. Divide the apple filling among the piecrusts, mounding the mixture in the center of each round.

11. Fold each piecrust over so the top layer of crust is about an inch short of the bottom layer. (The edges should not meet.) Use the back of a fork to seal the edges.

12. Insert the crisper plate into the basket and the basket into the unit. Preheat the unit by selecting AIR FRY, setting the temperature to 204°C, and setting the time to 3 minutes. Select START/STOP to begin.

13. Once the unit is preheated, spray the crisper plate with cooking oil, line the basket with baking paper, and spray it with cooking oil. Working in batches, place the hand pies into the basket in a single layer.

14. Select AIR FRY, set the temperature to 204°C, and set the time to 10 minutes. Select START/STOP to begin.

15. When the cooking is complete, let the hand pies cool for 5 minutes before removing from the basket.

16. Repeat steps 13, 14, and 15 with the remaining pies.

Gingerbread

Prep time: 5 minutes | Cook time: 20 minutes | Makes 1 loaf

INGREDIENTS

Cooking spray
¾ teaspoon ground ginger
½ teaspoon baking soda
60 g molasses or treacle
1 teaspoon pure vanilla extract
125 g plain flour
¼ teaspoon cinnamon
⅛ teaspoon salt
125 ml buttermilk
2 tablespoons sugar
1 teaspoon baking powder
1 egg
2 tablespoons oil

DIRECTIONS

1. Preheat the air fryer to 164°C.

2. Spray a baking dish lightly with cooking spray.

3. In a medium bowl, mix together all the dry ingredients.

4. In a separate bowl, beat the egg. Add molasses, buttermilk, oil, and vanilla and stir until well mixed.

5. Pour liquid mixture into dry ingredients and stir until well blended.

6. Pour batter into baking dish and bake at 164°C for 20 minutes or until toothpick inserted in center of loaf comes out clean.

Lime Bars

Prep time: 10 minutes | Cook time: 33 minutes | Makes 12 bars

INGREDIENTS

185 g blanched finely ground almond flour, divided
4 tablespoons salted butter, melted
2 large eggs, whisked

95 g powdered sweetener, divided
125 ml fresh lime juice

DIRECTIONS

1. In a medium bowl, mix together 125 g flour, 30 g sweetener, and butter. Press mixture into bottom of an ungreased round nonstick cake pan.
2. Place pan into air fryer basket. Adjust the temperature to 148°C and bake for 13 minutes. Crust will be brown and set in the middle when done.
3. Allow to cool in pan 10 minutes.
4. In a medium bowl, combine remaining flour, remaining sweetener, lime juice, and eggs. Pour mixture over cooled crust and return to air fryer for 20 minutes at 148°C. Top will be browned and firm when done.
5. Let cool completely in pan, about 30 minutes, then chill covered in the refrigerator 1 hour. Serve chilled.

Bananas Foster

Prep time: 5 minutes | Cook time: 7 minutes | Serves 2

INGREDIENTS

1 tablespoon unsalted butter
1 banana, peeled and halved lengthwise and then crosswise
⅛ teaspoon ground cinnamon
Vanilla ice cream, for serving

2 teaspoons dark brown sugar
2 tablespoons chopped pecans
2 tablespoons light rum

DIRECTIONS

1. In a baking pan, combine the butter and brown sugar. Place the pan in the air fryer basket. Set the air fryer to 176°C for 2 minutes, or until the butter and sugar are melted. Swirl to combine.
2. Add the banana pieces and pecans, turning the bananas to coat. Set the air fryer to 176°C for 5 minutes, turning the banana pieces halfway through the cooking time. Sprinkle with the cinnamon.
3. Remove the pan from the air fryer and place on an unlit stovetop for safety. Add the rum to the pan, swirling to combine it with the butter mixture. Carefully light the sauce with a long-reach lighter. Spoon the flaming sauce over the banana pieces until the flames die out.
4. Serve the warm bananas and sauce over vanilla ice cream.

Frozen Air Fryer Pancakes

Total time: 6 minutes | Cooking time: 6 minutes   Serving: 100 g or 6

INGREDIENTS

Pack of 6 frozen pancakes

Optional chocolate sauce

Optional toffee sauce

DIRECTIONS

Remove the packaging of frozen pancakes and place them into basket of air fryer. Ensure that you are not stacking them.

Air fryer the pancakes at 160 degree Celsius or 320 degrees Fahrenheit for 4 minutes.

Turn over the pancakes and air fryer them again at same temperature for 2 minutes more.

Serve them with your favorite sauce.

Air fryer Banana Souffle:

Total time: 18 minutes | Preparation time: 3 minutes | Cooking time: 15 minutes   Serving: 4

INGREDIENTS

2 medium sized bananas

2 large eggs

Extra virgin oil for spraying

½ tsp cinnamon

DIRECTIONS

Peel the bananas and add them to blender. Add eggs to them.

Add cinnamon to the blender and pulse until it gets smooth.

Use extra virgin oil to spray ramekins.

Put soufflé better into ramekins and place them in air fryer.

Air fryer the batter at 180 degrees Celsius or 360 degrees Fahrenheit for 15 minutes.

Serve the soufflés quickly before they start to fall.

Grilled Air Fryer Peaches:

Total time: 19 minutes | Preparation time: 5 minutes | Cooking time: 14 minutes Serving: 2

INGREDIENTS

Fresh peaches 4

1 tbsp honey

2 tsp butter

1 tsp ground ginger

Peach cobbler

DIRECTIONS

Slice the peaches and put them in air fryer basket.

Spray the sliced peaches with extra virgin oil.

Air fryer the peaches at 200 degrees Celsius or 400 degrees Fahrenheit for 8 minutes.

Place peach cobbler topping in a bowl and break it until it gains texture like breadcrumbs.

Remove the sliced peaches from air fryer and place them on a foil.

Now sprinkle the peaches with ginger and drizzle them with honey.

Now add butter and cobbler topping on peaches.

Place them back into air fryer at 200 degrees Celsius or 400 degrees Fahrenheit for 6 minutes.

On beeping, remove grilled peaches from air fryer and serve them with cream.

Printed in Great Britain
by Amazon